Converting a
Quality Management System using the
Process Approach

David Hoyle

John Thompson

Transition Support

A flexible approach to business improvement

Published by:-
Transition Support Ltd
Royal Monnow
Redbrook Road
Monmouth
Monmouthshire
NP25 3LY
Tel/Fax: 00 44 01600 716509
E-mail mail@transition-support.com
Web site http://www.transition-support.com

ISBN 1-903417-01-5

Printed in Wales by Copyplus Monmouth Tel: 00 44 1600 772600

Contents

**The past has only got us to
where we are today
:....*it may not necessarily get
us to where we want to be!*

Foreword

Since 1987 the policies and practices of organizations that serve the achievement of quality have been inextricably linked with ISO 9000 which has become the most successful international standard ever.

Organizations were being told that all they had to do was "document what you do and do what you document". This simplistic and often misleading message spread so widely that probably over 90% of the quality systems developed since 1987, are merely collections of documents describing what organizations believed was needed to satisfy the 20 elements of the standard. This approach to quality system development became known as the 'element' or 'clause' approach. Its focus was on conformity to requirements, often quite independently of business needs. As a consequence many organizations failed to realize any significant business benefit.

In the year 2000 revision of the ISO 9000 family of standards a fundamental change has taken place. The family of standards is now based on eight principles of quality management that align well with the criteria in the EFQM Excellence Model. Completely rewritten and now clearly focusing on customers, the 'do what you say - say what you do' approach and the 20 elements have been swept aside, to be replaced with 5 sections that better reflect how organizations operate. But perhaps the most significant change is that of a process approach to quality management. Requirements for documented procedures have almost disappeared now being replaced with requirements for processes. 'Process' is not just another word for 'procedure' but a totally different concept. The focus is now on the mechanisms in an organization that enable it to satisfy customers - these are the organization's 'business processes'. This presents a significant opportunity for organizations to achieve real business benefits through ISO 9000:2000.

For those organizations that designed their systems and behaviours around the 20 elements of the standard there will need to be significant change. Existing quality management systems will need to be converted so that they reflect a process approach to quality management.

The purpose of this guide is therefore to help these organizations convert their existing systems of documentation into systems of managed processes that deliver real business benefits.

How to use this book

Each chapter in the book deals with a separate topic and each one has a set of learning outcomes that can be accomplished by covering its contents. Chapter 1 should be read first as it provides the basis for understanding the approach taken by the ISO 9000:2000 family of standards. As many quality management systems will consist of a collection of procedures it is important that the reader gains an understanding of the difference between procedures and processes and hence Chapter 2 should be read next.

Chapter 3 provides an overview of the conversion process while chapters 4 to 8 cover the detail of the conversion process. Chapter 7 is the most comprehensive in the book, explaining process analysis and the factors that need to be taken into account when designing and constructing effective processes. Chapter 9 can be used at any stage in the conversion process as it contains criteria for judging a successful conversion and tracking progress.

Each chapter addresses the change in direction brought about by the ISO 9000:2000 family of standards. At the end of each chapter a summary is presented often in terms of the differences between the old approach and the new approach so as to continually emphasise the change in direction presented by the ISO 9000:2000 family of standards.

References to ISO 9000

Within this book reference to ISO 9000 without a year identifier refers to the old version of the family of standards unless a comparison is being made, when the form 'ISO 9000:1994' is used to denote the old family and 'ISO 9000:2000' to denote the new family of standards. Reference to the 'ISO 9000:2000 family' means ISO 9000, ISO 9001, ISO 9004 and ISO 19011 and it is therefore recommended that as a minimum, both ISO 9000 and ISO 9004 should be studied as well as ISO 9001 in preparing for the conversion. 'ISO 9000:2000' refers the Fundamentals and vocabulary standard. 'ISO 9001:2000' refers to the Requirements standard used for assessment and contractual purposes and 'ISO 9004:2000' refers to the Guidelines for performance improvement. ISO 19011 refers to the Quality and environmental system audit standard planned for released in 2001.

Chapter 1.

A real change in direction

Learning outcomes

After studying this chapter you should be able to:-

❑ understand the real change in direction of the new standard

❑ understand the reasons for change

❑ recognize the difference between system conformance and system performance

❑ explain the linkage between the role of the QMS and business outputs

A system focused on achieving business objectives

The ISO 9000:2000 family of standards is based on the process approach to management. This approach recognizes that all work is performed to achieve some objective. Also that the objective is achieved more efficiently when related resources and activities are managed as a process. In addition it is believed that the objectives of the organization which serve to meet its mission will be met more effectively when the organization is managed as a system of interrelated processes.

It follows therefore that this system should be designed to enable the organization to meet its objectives and should interconnect all the processes required to deliver the desired results. Objectives are derived from the expectations of interested parties as now referred to in the standard. Who are these interested parties? These for most organizations include:-

❑ Customers who want products and services that fulfil their expectations

❑ Suppliers who want commercially viable and stable relationships

❑ Employees who want satisfying employment

❑ Shareholders who want a good return on their investment

❑ Society that wants organizations to operate responsibly, lawfully and ethically

1

None of these interested parties or stakeholders have objectives that are unrelated to the others and therefore they cannot have systems that operate independently - in fact there can only be one system. The process approach is therefore concerned with managing the interrelationships between the interested parties so that all are satisfied - not just customers. It is not a trade-off. Employee satisfaction or care for society or the environment cannot traded-off against customer satisfaction. Clearly this is a change in focus and direction.

The fork in the road ~ old versus new interpretation

On first reading, the new standard can be interpreted as shown in the Customer fulfilment cycle (Figure 1.1). Here there is a clear linkage between quality policy, objectives and where the QMS delivers the outputs to satisfy customer needs. To many this does not represent a significant change from how a QMS has been perceived. In reality the QMS was only a system of documentation focused on conformity to procedures as shown in the Conformity cycle (Figure 1.2). Here the linkage is between procedures which implement quality policy and deliver records that demonstrate conformity, often independent of business objectives. What the new standard requires is to go beyond conformity and seek customer satisfaction. However, because of the interdependencies referred to above, we have to go even further, beyond *customer* satisfaction and seek satisfaction of *all* the interested parties.

The new standard needs to be interpreted as representing a QMS focused upon achieving business objectives as shown in the Business management cycle (Figure 1.3). Here the linkage is between a system of processes focused on achieving business objectives and satisfying the expectations of interested parties.

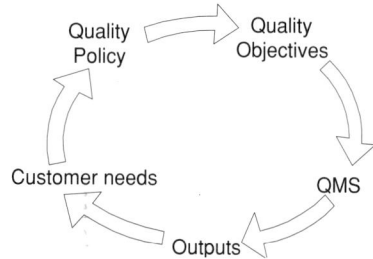

Figure 1.1 Customer fulfilment

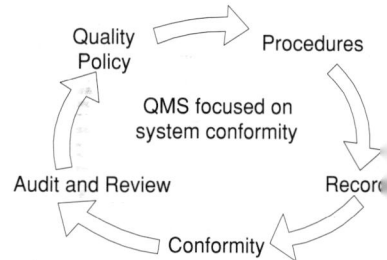

Figure 1.2 Conformity cycle

Figure 1.3 Business management cycle

Figure 1.4 Convergence towards business management cycle

What is important to perceive and understand is the fundamental difference between figures 1.2 and 1.3 and to interpret the changes to ISO 9000 as moving towards the Business management cycle and not a continuance of the Conformity cycle as illustrated in Figure 1.4. This view of a QMS clearly changes perceptions from a collection of procedures to the integration of business processes that involve people, technology, materials, equipment, facilities and the physical and human environment. However, it is the culture that drives the effectiveness of such systems and therefore no approach will be successful without taking full account of the prevailing culture in the organization. Whether the system is being developed from scratch or being converted from an established system, the development process is the same. The real differences emerge during system design, construction and operation. To convert a system that has been documented as a quality manual and a series of procedures firstly requires an understanding of the difference between procedures and processes.

What an ISO 9000:2000 organisation will look like

An organization that has embraced the process management approach will be able to demonstrate a number of role model characteristics:-

❏ A clearly defined business planning process that produces a robust business plan

❏ A business plan that consists of objectives, appropriate measures of success, actions focused on achieving those objectives with the relevant resources and skills provided

❑ An improvement culture and investment programme to support continual improvement objectives

❑ Measured and monitored performance improvements in financial, quality and customer satisfaction indicators

❑ Effective customer and market research processes linked to improvement planning

❑ Benchmarked performance against appropriate external data

❑ Awareness of position relative to competitor with known strengths and weaknesses

❑ Personnel development processes focused on releasing full potential

❑ Effective management of process

Summary

Clearly there is a real change in direction that results from comparing the old approach to ISO 9000, with its focus on system conformity, with the new approach with its focus on achieving real business benefits. The key differences in the two approaches are summarised in Table 1.1.

This chapter has explained the nature of the change, in a way that should initiate a change in perception about a QMS and give some insight into the magnitude of the change that lies ahead. In the next chapter, the difference between processes and procedures is explained in order to impart an understanding essential for a successful conversion to be accomplished.

Table 1.1 Contrast between old and new approaches

Old approach	New approach
No clearly defined and communicated organizational purpose and objectives	Everyone understands the organization's purpose and objectives and is motivated and supported to achieve them
No marketing process and customer satisfaction measurement within QMS	Marketing process integrated in QMS and customer satisfaction regularly monitored
People are just another resource to be used to achieve the results	People are valued and results achieved through team work
There is a set of random task based procedures that are independent of the business objectives	Processes are designed to meet defined objectives and are continually measured, reviewed and improved
The system for achieving quality is organized around the 20 elements of ISO 9001:1994	Processes are integrated into a coherent management system that is used to deliver business results
Continuous improvement is perceived as correcting mistakes only	Continuous improvement is perceived as proactively seeking opportunities to improve performance
Data generated by the QMS is not used to make decisions	Decisions are based on process performance data generated by the management system
Purchasing decisions are primarily based on lowest price	Key suppliers are involved in future strategy

Chapter 2.

Processes versus procedures

Learning outcomes

After studying this chapter you should be able to:-

❑ distinguish between procedures and processes

❑ understand what makes processes fundamentally different from procedures

❑ identify whether you have documented your procedures or your processes

❑ understand how big a gap exists between a procedural approach and a process approach

Change in direction

ISO 9001:1994 refers to documented procedures being required to implement almost every clause of the standard. In ISO 9001:2000, not only has the requirement for documented procedures been completely removed apart from a few specific instances but the requirement for documentation has also been drastically reduced, signalling a change in direction away from documentation as the primary output from implementing ISO 9001:2000. The emphasis has moved from documented procedures to defined processes where the degree of documentation required is determined from an analysis of need. However, this change in direction as indicated in the Foreword and Chapter 1, is much more than a change in words. Procedures are not documented processes - as will be become apparent from reading this chapter.

Procedures

Within the context of quality management standards, and more specifically ISO 9000, 'procedure' was a key word which acquired a particular meaning over the years. In its simplest form a procedure is a way in which one works to accomplish a task. It can therefore be a sequence of steps that include preparation, conduct and completion of a task. Each step can be a sequence of activities and each activity a sequence of actions. The sequence of steps is critical to whether a statement or document is a procedure or something else. Specifications, contracts and records are not procedures as they do not tell us how to do anything. These describe the outputs resulting from carrying out procedures or tasks, leaving us to decide any further actions necessary to utilize these outputs. The output will more than likely be used as input to other procedures.

We need procedures when the task we have to perform is complex or when the task is routine and we want it to be performed consistently. Hence procedures are intended to make something happen in a certain way. If we are not concerned about how something is done and are interested only in the result we do not produce procedures but issue instructions such as 'post the letter', 'repair the spin drier' or 'recruit another person'. These are work instructions as they intend us to do 'quantitative' work without telling us how to do it or the 'qualitative' standard to which the work should be carried out. Instructions are therefore not procedures unless they follow in a sequence and enable us to perform a task.

A set of self-assembly instructions is a procedure as it tells how to proceed to assemble the product. But the wording on the label telling us not to put hot objects on the surface is an instruction or a warning (a special type of instruction). As procedures are normally used by people they are designed with a user in mind. The user is normally an individual or a group of individuals, although procedures can cover a sequence of steps, each of which is performed by different individuals or groups. However, perceptions of procedures vary considerably depending on the context in which they are created and used.

Any sequence of steps, no matter how simple or complex, can be expressed as a procedure that is intended to cause someone to act in a certain way to accomplish a task. The key is that the steps follow a sequence. A random collection of statements is not a procedure unless they are rearranged in a sequence that enables someone to proceed.

Misleading labels

Within the context of a QMS (and more specifically, ISO 9000) the procedure has, for many, taken on particular and sometimes peculiar characteristics. Such (documented) procedures may be written not as a sequence of activities or steps but as a series of requirements or a series of responsibilities. Neither of these can be procedures as they do not tell us how to proceed, what steps to take or how to measure the result.

Such procedures often follow a uniform format with a purpose statement, applicability statement, responsibilities and then procedure statements. Often there is no connection between the purpose statement and the procedure. Purpose statements often address the purpose of a document not the purpose of the task that the sequence of tasks is intended to deliver. Again, if such procedures (and rarely they do) contain measures of success, these are probably quantitative measures related to the task itself and not to why the procedure is carried out. The most common perception of such procedures is that they are simply associated with paperwork and filling in forms.

We seem to think that we have created a procedure by classifying a document as a procedure. These documents are often thought of as high-level procedures. Procedures do not have to be documented to be procedures and do not have to be high level. We often hear of procedures addressing the 20 elements of ISO 9000 and work instructions being used at departmental level to guide activities. These characteristics of procedures only serve to constrain our thoughts and our intent.

Processes

Processes convert inputs into outputs. They create a change of state. They take inputs (e.g. material, information, people) and pass these through a sequence of stages during which the inputs are transformed or their status changed to emerge as an output with different characteristics. Hence processes act upon inputs and are dormant until the input is received. At each stage the transformation tasks may be procedural, but may also be mechanical, chemical etc. Inherent processes do not normally recognise departmental or functional boundaries (but are often hindered by them) nor the boundaries between customers and suppliers. Each process has an objective with both quantitative and qualitative measures of its outputs, directly related to its objectives. The transformation or process stages are designed to ensure the combination of resources achieves the objectives - the desired outputs. Of course this means that the process has to receive the right inputs to deliver the desired outputs and that the correct resources are applied at the right stages, in the correct quantities and in the right manner. It is true that a process can be illustrated as a sequence of steps just as a procedure is illustrated, but the similarity ends there.

Semantics

The way we use the words procedure and process tells us something about how they differ. We tend to start and stop processes. We implement procedures and commence and complete them. We process information. We do not procedure information but we may employ a procedure to process information. We have plating processes and there may be plating procedures. In this context, the plating process comprises the resources, people, plant and machinery, and the plating procedure contains the instructions on how to plate material.

We have process interrupt but not procedure interrupt, because processes are perceived as continuous and run until physical intervention. In our bodies we have processes, not procedures. The reproductive process, the digestive process, the respiratory process, these processes are certainly continuous and stop only when an intervention takes place. They may require human intervention in which a surgeon may employ procedures to effect a repair. Procedures on the other hand are perceived as being discontinuous, having steps which can be paused with activities or actions picked up or put down at will.

Procedures usually relate to groups of activities with a given output where that output may not be complete until acted upon by someone else at a later stage in the process. Therefore, procedures are the actions taken by individuals in a process that may span across several functions and use multiple resources to deliver a predetermined output at a given rate at a given location on a given date.

It should be clear by now that procedures are intended for use by people and are a product of the command and control age. It was believed that prescribing what people were required to do resulted in people doing the right things right first time. It was not appreciated that all work is a process and in addition to the commands, the required outputs will only be realized if the people have:-

❑   the ability to do the job

❑   the motivation to do the job

❑   the resources to do the job

Where processes primarily differ from procedures is that processes are dynamic and procedures are static. Processes are dependent upon resources and the ability and motivation of the personnel involved to generate the desired outcome, whereas procedures are only a series of instructions for a person to follow.

Changing perceptions

Whether any change is necessary often depends upon one's current perception and attitude. If documented procedures merely respond to requirements in a standard they are not likely to demonstrate a clear line of sight to the real purpose of why the procedure is necessary. This is very often the root cause of why the people involved do not see the value in carrying out the actions. It is very likely that many organisations will have to undergo a fairly radical rethink of the way they regard their management system. In order to satisfy the requirements, needs and expectations of the interested parties (customers, shareholders, employees, suppliers and community) organisations have to identify the critical processes that deliver satisfaction. It is also clear that the effective management of those processes depends upon common understanding and monitoring of how success is measured. Perhaps the most crucial and radical factor is the constant focus and alignment of the key stages on achieving the end results.

The implication here is that in many cases the organisation and the activities must have a greater alignment. The previous notion of a 'functional' organisation (for example, where different departments have created their own internal agendas and cultures with no clear linkage to defined organisational objectives) has to be seriously questioned. It is all too tempting for organisations to address this issue by simply adopting a 'cross-functional' approach which in reality means that they gather together representatives from different functional bunkers and let them fight it out. In general, cross-functional teams are not a substitute for process management. Simplistically, functions tend to be vertical while processes are horizontal, with stakeholder interest at both ends.

To make a transition from managing procedures to process management, an organisation must answer whether it has:

❑	clearly defined what its objectives are and how it will measure and review the success of achieving these objectives

❑	evaluated the impact of those objectives on the interested parties, the stakeholders

❑	designed the critical, end-to-end processes necessary to deliver the objectives

❑	assessed and provided the resources, skills and competence to make the processes work

The underlying principles of the business excellence model and the changes to ISO 9000 should leave us in no doubt that the change in language from procedure to process is not about perception or semantics.

There is a very real change of focus required by many organisations if they are to remain competitive, and with this change comes the significant opportunity to ensure that their processes are designed to consistently add value.

Summary

In simple terms a procedure enables a task to be performed whereas a process enables a result to be achieved. This is the fundamental difference and should help the change in perception. Other ways of perceiving procedures and processes that are discussed in this chapter are indicated in Table 2.1. It is only when the difference in concept has been realized that the whole perception of a QMS will change and that the change is not simply a change of words.

Table 2.1 Contrast between procedures and processes

Procedures	**Processes**
Procedures are driven by completion of the task	Processes are driven by achievement of a desired output
Procedures are implemented	Processes are operated
Procedure steps completed by different people in different departments with different objectives	Process stages are completed by different people with the same objectives - departments do not matter
Procedures are discontinuous	Processes flow to conclusion
Procedures focus on satisfying the rules	Processes focus on satisfying the stakeholders
Procedures define the sequence of steps to execute a task	Processes transform inputs into outputs through use of resources
Procedures are driven by humans	Processes are driven by physical forces some of which may be human
Procedures may be used to process information	Information is processed by use of a procedure
Procedures exist - they are static	Processes behave - they are dynamic
Procedures cause people to take actions and decisions	Processes cause things to happen

From reading Chapters 1 and 2, a clear understanding of the nature and magnitude of the change should now be forming. Anyone approaching the conversion process should read these two chapters before proceeding further - to do otherwise will run the risk of carrying the baggage of an obsolete approach into the new era and thus jeopardise the success of the conversion.

Chapter 3.

The Conversion process

Learning outcomes

After studying this chapter you should be able to:-

☐ understand the difference between the 'document what you do' approach and the 'process' approach to system development

☐ understand the steps to be taken to convert element-based systems to process-based systems

☐ identify the factors that affect success in the conversion process

☐ understand how application of the process approach to system conversion differs from the 'document what you do' approach

Change in direction

ISO 9001:1994 required a quality system to be established, documented and maintained and the system and its documented procedures effectively implemented. ISO 9001:2000 requires a quality management system to be established, documented, implemented, maintained and continuously improved. While the obvious difference is the inclusion of the requirement for continuous improvement, the additional requirements on establishing the QMS go far beyond the notion that a QMS is a set of documents. There are requirements for the processes to be identified, their sequence and interaction determined, criteria and methods for their effective operation determined and process measurement, monitoring, analysis and improvement performed. These requirements signal a fundamental change in direction. They indicate that the 'document what you do' approach would be an inappropriate approach to take. The QMS has to be designed to achieve planned results i.e. business objectives - not simply conformity with procedures. The QMS is still required to be established and documented, but in view of what the QMS is now required to achieve we need to re-examine what "to establish" and "documented" really mean.

Previously, "to establish" was often interpreted as meaning "putting in place the documented procedures". In order to establish a "system" it has to be put in place and putting a "system" in place (rather than just a collection of procedures) requires several separate actions (assuming that we understand that a system is the totality of concepts, principles, resources, information, people and processes required to achieve defined objectives).

Previously "documented" was often interpreted as meaning that everything needed to be written down but this caused considerable difficulties in knowing what to document. This was because of a conflict between the business need for documentation and the need to demonstrate conformity to external auditors. The ISO 9000:2000 family of standards recognizes that documentation should exist primarily to achieve business objectives.

The system firstly needs to be designed (to meet the defined objectives) after which it needs to be installed and commissioned before it can be considered operational. The approach is very similar to building any system, be it an air-conditioning system, a political system or an education system. However, the system is not in place until it has been integrated into the fabric of the organization so that people do the right things right without being told - then, and only then, can it be claimed the system is in place. This is a different concept, one which requires a new approach to building a QMS. Although many reading this book will work in organizations with existing systems (not necessarily established systems!) the process of converting an existing system is not simply replacing documented procedures with a suite of flow charts, as will become apparent from reading this chapter.

Conversion process overview

The conversion of a QMS is a project with the objective of constructing a management system that enables an organization to achieve its objectives effectively and efficiently. The process commences with a need for change, which represents a gap between where we are and where we want to be. This is converted to a commitment to change when the climate is favourable and management is convinced of the need. A plan for change is developed and agreed for the conversion of the QMS into a system for achieving the new objectives. The conversion itself is an iterative process during which perceptions of the system are changed, the business processes identified, captured and analysed and changes introduced. Conversion is complete when the system delivers the desired results. This is illustrated in Figure 3.1 which shows in a figure-of-eight loop, how the current cycle is linked with the conversion cycle in a continuous process of improvement.

Quality Policy → Quality Objectives → Conversion → Plan for change → Commitment to change → Need for change → QMS → Outputs → Customer needs → Quality Policy

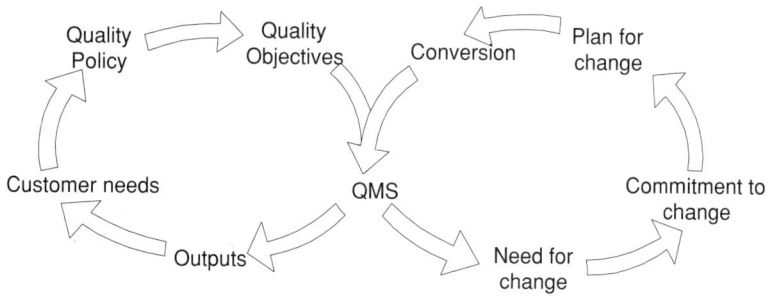

Figure 3.1 The conversion cycle

The conversion process itself comprises two sub-processes - system design and system construction. Once the new policy and objectives have been defined, system design can commence. The system design process is complete when all the processes have been defined and a process development plan has been produced that shows how the system will be constructed.

The need for change

As stated in the Foreword, perhaps as many as 90% of the ISO 9000 registered organizations will have adopted the 'element' or 'clause' approach to QMS design and therefore for these organizations to realize the business benefits from ISO 9001:2000, there is a compelling need for change. The change is about the way the QMS is perceived and managed, not necessarily about writing a completely new set of documents. Clearly, there will be some new documents to produce but equally there may be many more documents that are simply withdrawn as they serve no useful purpose. For those who have the task of convincing top management to invest in the change, it is important to convey that the QMS must be focused on delivering the planned business outputs, not simply on maintaining certification to ISO 9000 (although that may be their previous perception).

Commitment to change

The previous chapters provide the compelling reasons for change - what is needed is to present these in a manner that will convince top management to invest in the change. The first hurdle is to establish why a QMS is needed. While the initial reason may have been to obtain ISO 9000 certification because of customer pressure or marketing advantage, the purpose of a QMS is to enable the organization to meet its declared objectives. It should not be as was previously - to simply get ISO 9000 registration.

Part of the problem is the perception of the QMS. If the word Quality creates difficulties in winning the argument, don't use it. The system can still be compliant with ISO 9001:2000 if it called a Management System, a Business Management System or anything else. It is not what it is called that matters - it is what it accomplishes and that all parties recognize the system achieves business results and that they are part of it.

The second hurdle is getting buy-in from all parties concerned. Explaining that the system is about effective process management with the emphasis on business results and not about conformity to documented procedures should get total support.

Commitment is doing what you say you will do. However, it depends on the doers, knowing the right things to do and having a passion for the results they expect. One of the most common reasons why organizations encounter trouble 12-18 months after the initial ISO 9000 registration is a lack of commitment. They no longer do what they said they would do, but it is not because they are being deliberately dishonest - it is more likely they did not fully understand what the whole thing was about. Getting commitment is about creating a passion for the results and the road to commitment is often a six stage process as shown in Table 3.1. You may need to lead each person involved along this road before you have their commitment.

Table 3.1 The road to commitment

Stage	Level	Meaning
0	Zero	I don't know anything about it
1	Awareness	I know what it is and why I should do it
2	Understanding	I know what I have to do and what I need to do it
3	Investment	I have the resources to do it and I know how to deploy them
4	Intent	This is what I am going to do and how I am going to do it
5	Action	I have completed the first few actions and it has been successful
6	Commitment	I am now doing everything I said I would do

System design process

The System Design process is illustrated in Figure 3.2 indicating the tasks, inputs and outputs associated with its execution. Under the 'document what you do' approach, this phase would not have existed. Systems were not designed at all - whatever form the systems took - they were merely documented. The quality manual was a document that responded to the requirements of the standard and referenced the associated procedures, thus creating a system of documentation that mirrored the standard rather than the business. As the system is now perceived to comprise a series of interconnected processes that enable the organization to achieve its business objectives, it is now necessary to design a system to fulfil that specific purpose.

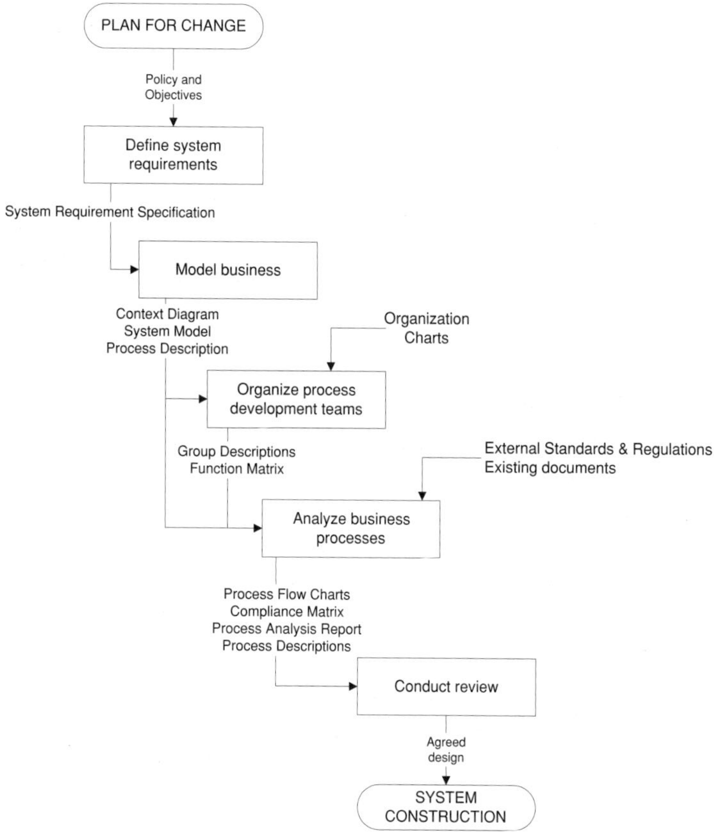

Figure 2 System design process

The System Design process commences with the development of a System Requirements Specification following which a model of the business is constructed in terms of its relationships with external interfaces and stakeholders. The core processes that deliver the organization's product should then be identified and these reviewed to ensure that no significant process has been overlooked.

Process Development Teams can be set up to carry out process analysis in order to identify the characteristics of each process. The primary output from the team is a suite of process flow charts that describe the sequence of task that transform business inputs into the desired business outputs.

The requirements of the external standards and regulations are deployed to the models in order to identify those current tasks that implement the requirements and those new tasks that need to be added to be compliant. Performance indicators and measurement methods are defined and the flow charts annotated to indicate the data collection points.

The results of the process analysis are documented and a series of process development plans prepared identifying all the changes required to enable the processes to meet the new objectives. The system design process ends when all the process models and development plans are agreed before proceeding to the System Construction Phase.

System construction

The system construction process is illustrated in Figure 3.3 indicating the principal stages that follow system design. Under the 'document what you do' approach, this phase would cover the documentation and implementation stages. System construction commences with release of the system design consisting of the process descriptions, process analysis report and process development plan.

The process descriptions contain details of the existing processes and the process analysis report identifies the information needs and recommended changes to be made to implement process management. The process development plan defines the stages through which the processes will be developed, the responsibilities and timescales for their completion.

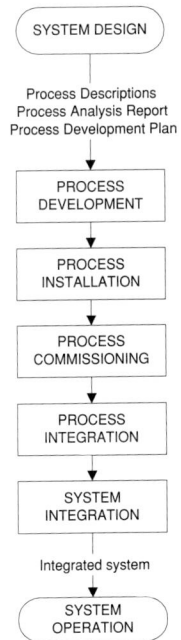

```
    ( SYSTEM DESIGN )

      Process Descriptions
      Process Analysis Report
      Process Development Plan
               │
               ▼
        ┌──────────────┐
        │   PROCESS    │
        │ DEVELOPMENT  │
        └──────────────┘
               │
               ▼
        ┌──────────────┐
        │   PROCESS    │
        │ INSTALLATION │
        └──────────────┘
               │
               ▼
        ┌──────────────┐
        │   PROCESS    │
        │ COMMISSIONING│
        └──────────────┘
               │
               ▼
        ┌──────────────┐
        │   PROCESS    │
        │ INTEGRATION  │
        └──────────────┘
               │
               ▼
        ┌──────────────┐
        │    SYSTEM    │
        │ INTEGRATION  │
        └──────────────┘
               │
         Integrated system
               │
               ▼
        (   SYSTEM    )
        (  OPERATION  )
```

Figure 3.3 Construction process

17

In the past, this process has been referred to as document development or simply implementation but these terms underestimate the work involved. Establishing an effective QMS means setting up a system on a permanent basis and putting it in place so that it functions effectively.

Following their design, the processes of the system need to be resourced, installed, commissioned and integrated into the fabric of the organization before it can be claimed that a system is in place. In order to construct the processes, information needs are matched with existing documentation and new information documented. Unlike the 'document what you do' approach, the information describing processes forms a coherent set so that all components of the system are described.

Process installation proceeds in parallel with process development so that new and revised practices are put in place at the same time as changes are being made in the cultural environment. The Installation stage involves decommissioning old processes, preparing new foundations and installing new processes. The system needs to be constructed upon firm foundations and without the appropriate culture in place, the foundations will not be sound enough to enable processes to operate effectively. This was one of the weaknesses with the 'document what you do' approach - it did not change the culture and hence did not create conditions for improved performance. Merely documenting current practice would only formalize it and run the risk of making it more difficult to change if not in practice; the perception that its now 'cast in concrete' often prevailed.

Following installation, processes are commissioned. This involves training the people, running the processes, analysing the results and fine-tuning the processes so that performance reaches the level required. During this stage, the monitoring components are activated, data is collected and performance evaluated.

After commissioning there follows a prolonged period during which the processes are integrated into the fabric of the organization. Process integration is not so much about integrating quality, health, safety and environmental aspects, but about changing behaviour so that people do the right things right without having to be told. The steps within a process become routine, habits are formed and beliefs strengthened. The way people act and react to certain stimulus becomes predictable and produces results that are predictable. System construction is complete when integration has taken place

Summary

The conversion process is about changing the mind set from the 'document what you do' approach to the process approach. The new approach treats the QMS as a dynamic system that is integrated into the fabric of the organization and not a set of documents that are brought out just before the auditors arrive, dusted and updated. Differences in the approach are illustrated in Table 3.2.

Table 3.2 Contrast between two approaches to QMS management

Document what you do approach	Process approach
Establish a QMS in response to customer pressure	Establish a QMS as a means to accomplish the organization's goals
Produce procedures as required by the standard	Design a system of interconnected processes that reflects the operations of the business
Produce a quality manual that responds to the standard	Produce a system description that describes how business objectives are achieved
Respond to the requirements of the standard	Respond to the needs of the business
Address the requirements of the standard in the order they are presented	Deploy the requirements of the standard onto the business
Document the procedures	Document the processes
Issue the procedures	Commission processes
Implement procedures	Integrate processes into the fabric of the organization

This chapter has summarised the conversion process so as to provide an insight into what lies ahead. The next stage is to form a vision of where the organization wants to be and plan for the change as will be explained in the next chapter.

Chapter 4.

Planning for change

Learning outcomes

After studying this chapter you should be able to:-

❑ define the vision for the QMS in realistic terms

❑ understand how the quality management principles can be used to redefine the quality policy

❑ reassess the quality policy using the quality management principles

❑ define objectives for the organization that directly serve the mission statement

❑ establish the scope of the new QMS

❑ determine the characteristics of the QMS that will enable it to meet the defined objectives

Change in direction

ISO 9001:1994 required the policy for quality, including objectives for quality and the commitment to quality to be defined and documented. There was no criteria given that would guide users in producing an effective quality policy. Typical implementation of this requirement led to "motherhood" policies that were often identical from one organization to another. The quality policy was often something that management declared without understanding what it meant and what relationship it had to business policies. The objectives for quality were often interpreted as being included within the same policy statement and thus were not perceived as something that was measured. It was not related to business objectives simply because the QMS was not perceived as central to business performance.

In the ISO 9000:2000 family there are five key changes here:

The meaning of quality - Quality now relates to the fulfilment of customers requirements as well as the requirements of other interested parties - a significant change in direction from *products that satisfy stated or implied needs.*

Evidence of commitment - Top management are now required to provide evidence of commitment - not merely *define and document it* - clearly another change in direction.

The scope of the quality policy - This is required to address continuous improvement, customer requirements and regulatory and legal requirements and provide a framework for establishing the quality objectives - another marked change in direction away from "motherhood" statements of little use.

Quality objectives - These are required to be measurable and consistent with the quality policy.

Processes and resources - Those needed to achieve the quality objectives now have to be identified and planned - clearly a dramatic change in direction from *documented procedures in accordance with the requirements of the standard.*

This clear link between policy, objectives and the processes to achieve them signals a fundamental change in direction that will be apparent from reading this chapter.

Defining system requirements

Few endeavours are successful without a clear vision of what is to be accomplished. Often the vision can be held in the mind but when several people are involved in realizing the vision it is wise to write it down. With a well-constructed specification addressing the important issues, everyone involved will be left in no doubt as to what the organization is attempting to do.

Following a decision to go ahead with developing or converting a QMS, a System Requirement Specification should be prepared that addresses the following points:-

Quality policy

Quality policies that were written within the context of the Conformity cycle (see Figure 1.2) were more likely to be focused on the system itself and not related to the business.

The quality policy need not be seen as a separate entity from the organization's stated business policies which in some organizations are expressed as the vision, mission, values, strategy, intentions. In effect for simplicity, these expressions constitute the organization's mission as indicated in Figure 1.3.

The eight quality management principles referred to in ISO 9000:2000 and identified in Table 4.1, could be used to test the mission. For example, how does the policy enable the organization to focus on its customers, how does it enable the involvement of people? Rather than repeating the words contained in the eight principles, business policies should be capable of demonstrating that they have been based on these principles. A mission that does not include commitments to continually improve its performance is unlikely to be robust.

Table 4.1 Quality management principles

Principle	Description
Customer focused organisation	Organisations depend on their customers and therefore should understand current and future customer needs, meet customer requirements and strive to exceed customer expectations.
Leadership	Leaders establish unity of purpose, direction, and the internal environment of the organisation. They create the environment in which people become fully involved in achieving the organisation's objectives.
Involvement of people	People at all levels are the essence of an organisation and their full involvement enables their abilities to be used for the organisation's benefit.
Process approach	A desired result is achieved more efficiently when related resources and activities are managed as a process.
System approach to management	Identifying, understanding and managing a system of interrelated processes for a given objective contributes to the effectiveness and efficiency of the organisation.
Continual improvement	Continual improvement is a permanent objective of the organisation.
Factual approach to decision making	Effective decisions are based on the logical and intuitive analysis of data and information.
Mutually beneficial supplier relationships	Mutually beneficial relationships between the organisation and its suppliers enhance the ability of both organisations to create value.

Business objectives

The business objectives should be derived directly from the mission statement and during the conversion process it is a good idea to capture these objectives in the System Requirement Specification so that they act as constant reminder of the reason for the QMS.

There are two types of objectives: those that focus on results such as increasing sales, return on capital, profitability and those that focus on enablers that achieve these results such as, improving the competence of employees, reducing down-time of equipment, improving customer communication.

The eight quality management principles could be used to test the business objectives. This could for example involve an assessment to test the presence of:-

❏ Objectives for maintaining or improving customer focus relative to marketing, social responsibility and human resources

❏ Objectives for maintaining or improving leadership relative to marketing, innovation and human resources

❏ Objectives for maintaining or improving the involvement of people in all areas or specific areas

❏ Objectives for maintaining or improving the productivity of specific processes

❏ Objectives for maintaining or improving the processes by which continual improvement is accomplished in marketing, innovation, supply chain management

❏ Objectives for maintaining or improving the integrity of data used in making marketing decisions, innovation decisions, productivity decisions etc

❏ Objectives for maintaining or improving relationships with suppliers used in the marketing, innovation and production functions

In order to quantify these objectives the current performance in each of these areas needs to establish and targets chosen that are challenging but attainable.

System scope

The scope of the system has in the past been related to what the organization required to be covered by its ISO 9000 certificate of registration. The very nature of the certification process allowed organizations to 'cherry pick' the parts of their organization that were perceived as directly related to the standard.

This led to obvious anomalies for example, design, servicing and distribution functions being excluded from the certificated system where clearly these functions were vital to satisfying customer requirements. In the new standard, the scope of the system is the scope of the business. A QMS meeting ISO 9001:2000 will embrace marketing, invoicing, human resources, facility maintenance, distribution and any other function that contributes towards the achievement of the business objectives. Therefore for most organizations, this will mean a radical change as the scope of the QMS is redefined.

System design criteria

Clearly the QMS must enable the organization to achieve its objectives and the organization needs to determine what will affect its ability to do this. These are the factors that constitute a robust design. A business that relies on a rapid response must have a system that provides a rapid response not one that is lethargic. A high-tech business may need to constantly change its products and its organization, therefore it must have a system that is not constrained by who does what and where they fit in the organization.

To determine these design criteria, try completing this sentence for the current organization:

"We need a system that........

Some examples are:-

❑ We need a system that does not constrain us to the way we are currently organized. We need freedom!

❑ We need a system that encourages us to seek and use best practice.

❑ We need a system that is integrated into the fabric of the organization.

❑ We need a well defined system that will drive us towards our goals.

❑ We need a system that enables us to anticipate events.

❑ We need a system to enable us to predict our performance.

❑ We need a system that will prevent disruptions in business continuity.

❑ We need a system that enables us to control technological change and organizational change.

❑ We need a system that will give our Customers confidence that we will meet their needs and expectations.

Summary

Without a clear vision of what is to be accomplished no endeavour will be successful. Therefore in the conversion programme it is important to set out with clearly defined goals and for everyone to understand the reason why a QMS is needed. The differences between the traditional approach and approach to quality policy and objectives are summarised in Table 4.2.

As a result of the consolidation of the three assessment standards (ISO 9001, 2 & 3 into ISO 9001:2000) the scope of the QMS can no longer omit key activities of the business. Organizations will now have to include all activities and this will mean a radical change as they redefine the scope of the QMS.

Table 4.2 Contrasting old and new approach to policy and objectives

Old approach	New approach
Define quality policy	Define the organization's mission
Ensure the quality policy looks like all others	Use the 8 QM principles to test the mission statement
Include quality objectives in quality policy	Derive measurable business objectives directly from the mission
Forget about quality objectives and focus on conformity with procedures	Use the 8 QM principles to test the business linkage and completeness of objectives
Include within the QMS only those functions that directly service customer orders	Include every process and hence every function within the QMS - exclude none
No obvious connection between quality policy, objectives and procedures	Clear linkage between mission, objectives and processes

Once the vision of where the organization wants to be has been established, work can commence on modelling the business as will be explained in the next chapter.

Chapter 5.

Modelling the business

Learning outcomes

After studying this chapter you should be able to:-

❏ construct a model of the business that identifies the key processes and their interfaces

❏ understand the nature of business processes and how they differ from functional activities

❏ understand the importance of the linkages between business processes and how to make the connections

❏ describe each of the business processes in terms that will facilitate their analysis and development

Change in direction

ISO 9001:1994 required a quality manual to be prepared covering the requirements of the standard and documented procedures to be prepared consistent with the requirements of the standard. This led to the approach of picking up the standard, paraphrasing the requirements in a manual and translating them directly into procedures. The result was a standard-led system that bore little relationship to the way business was conducted. The change in direction described in Chapter 4, clearly demonstrates that a new approach is now necessary - an approach that puts the business at the centre and the standard in the role of providing a supporting framework - not the driver and no longer in the centre.

Who should do this?

Because the QMS has to be central to the business, top management are by default the system designers. It is therefore important that they are brought together as a team to share their perceptions of how the business is and should be managed to achieve its objectives. The management team should derive a common picture of the business. This picture can be represented by two models - a context diagram and system model.

The context diagram

Having defined a clear vision of what is to be accomplished, a diagram should be produced to place the organization in context with its stakeholders and their requirements and expectations. This can be referred to as a context diagram an example of which is illustrated in Figure 5.1

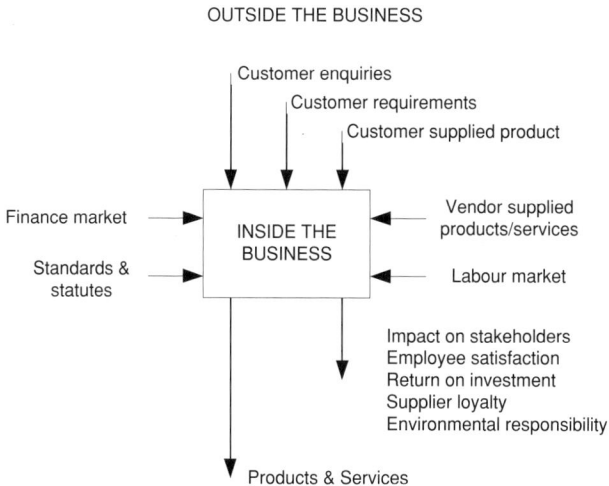

OUTSIDE THE BUSINESS

Customer enquiries
Customer requirements
Customer supplied product

Finance market → INSIDE THE BUSINESS ← Vendor supplied products/services

Standards & statutes → ← Labour market

Impact on stakeholders
Employee satisfaction
Return on investment
Supplier loyalty
Environmental responsibility

Products & Services

Figure 5.1 Context diagram

The interfaces should include three type of inputs:

a)   the customers that provide requirements and/or product for processing

b)   external organizations that provide product or information to accomplish the mission

c)   internal organizations (but external to that part of the organization for which the quality system is being developed) that provide product or information to accomplish the organization's mission

The outputs should be represented as outcomes of the business in terms of:-

d)　products and services supplied (the physical outputs)

e)　impacts on stakeholders (customers, employees, suppliers, investors, owners, society)

The result should be illustrated in a Context Diagram that shows where the organization fits in its environment. The specific product or information that passes along the channels that link the organization with its interfaces should also be specified.

These channels represent the principal channels of communication between the organization and its customers and suppliers. They provide the inputs and requirements for the result-producing processes within the organization.

The system model

From the Context Diagram a System Model should be developed that defines the core processes within the organization that convert the specified inputs into the required outputs. A System Model focused on the customer is shown in Figure 5.2. Other system models could be generated that focus on other stakeholders e.g. employees, suppliers, shareholders.

These core processes are known as Business Processes. In general these are 'end to end' series of activities that transform stakeholder needs into satisfaction. Everything that the organization does should fit into one or more of these processes so that they cover the organization's entire scope of work both operationally and administratively.

The impact of the organization on its stakeholders is not shown in the model primarily because it results from the behaviour of the participants and therefore emanates from every process.

In this generic model the core processes have the following characteristics.

Marketing process

The marketing process seeks out customer's current unfulfilled needs and expectations, translates these into the organization's capability and delivers potential customer's into the sales process. The process predicts customer future needs which are vital in the business management process to forming the organization's strategy. The marketing process also delivers new opportunities into the product/service generation process so that new products and services may be created to satisfy customer needs and expectations.

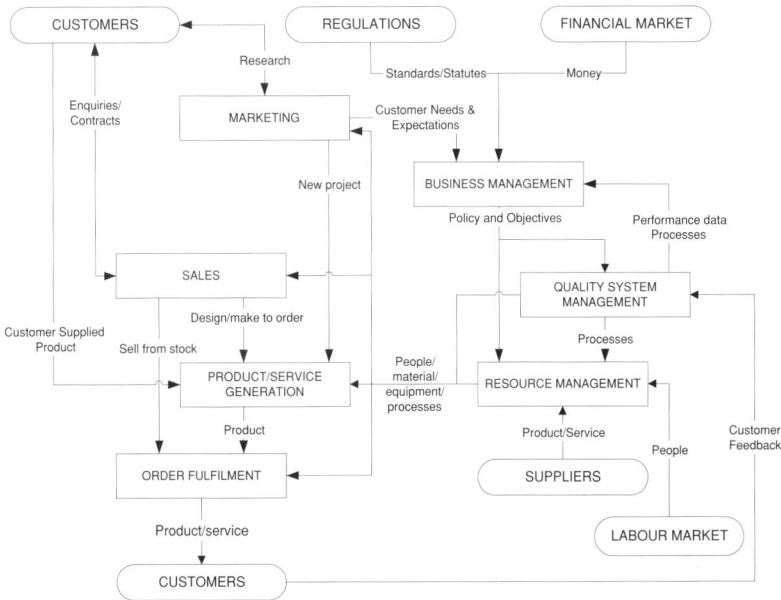

Figure 5.2 System model (customer focused)

Sales process

The sales process makes contact with customers for existing products and services. It handles customer enquiries, processes contracts/orders and delivers requirements into product/service generation processes or directly into the order-fulfilment process if product/service is already available for supply.

Product/service generation process

The product/service generation process transforms customer needs and expectations or specified requirements into products and services that satisfy customers. For existing product, this process replicates proven designs to consistent standards. For existing services, this process would involve the pre-service delivery processes such as planning. For new products/services, the requirements pass through a design process before emerging as a set of proven specifications that can be transformed into a tangible product/service. There are many variations within this process depending on the nature of the transaction between customer and supplier.

Order-fulfilment process

The order-fulfilment process supplies saleable product/service against customer requirements. In some cases the product may be in stock or the service operational. In other cases the product may need to have been specifically produced or a service specifically designed to fulfil a given order. For tangible product, this process would include sub-processes of storage, packing, dispatch, shipment, installation and invoicing.

For services, the order-fulfilment process equates to the service delivery process. For services with high tangible product content this may include maintenance and technical support. For services with low tangible product content, this may include consultations, health care, provision, investment services etc.

Business management process

The Business Management process creates the vision, the mission and the overall strategy for the organization. Taking market research data from the marketing process, external standards, laws and other constraints, this strategy delivers the policies and objectives for the organization to fulfil in order to create and retain satisfied customers. The business management process also monitors performance and manages both strategic and tactical changes to deliver the desired results for all stakeholders.

Resource management process

Triggered by the organization's objectives and requirements of specific customers, projects and initiatives, the resource management process equips, maintains and develops the human and physical resources needed to fulfil its objectives. It comprises several sub-processes concerned with resource planning, acquisition, deployment, maintenance and disposal. The resource would comprise people, products, materials, equipment, facilities and hence involve for example purchasing, personnel, plant maintenance and calibration services.

Quality system management process

The quality system management process provides the means to manage the interconnected processes that give the organization the capability to achieve its objectives. It then maintains, evaluates and improves the processes so that the organization maintains the capability to sustain customer satisfaction. By measuring, reviewing, evaluating and acting upon process and customer feedback the system and its performance are continually improved.

Naming the processes

The process names in Figure 5.2 are generic and not intended to equate with any particular function or department in an organization. Each organization would identify the business processes by names that accurately describe the process. Where a proposed process name is the same as the name of an organizational function, an alternative name for the process should be chosen to ensure that business processes remain multifunctional and not the sole responsibility of a single function.

It is important to recognize that many departments outside the sales and marketing departments participate in the sales and marketing process. The product/service generation process should be broken down into the key result-producing sub-processes such as product design, development, production, or service design etc.

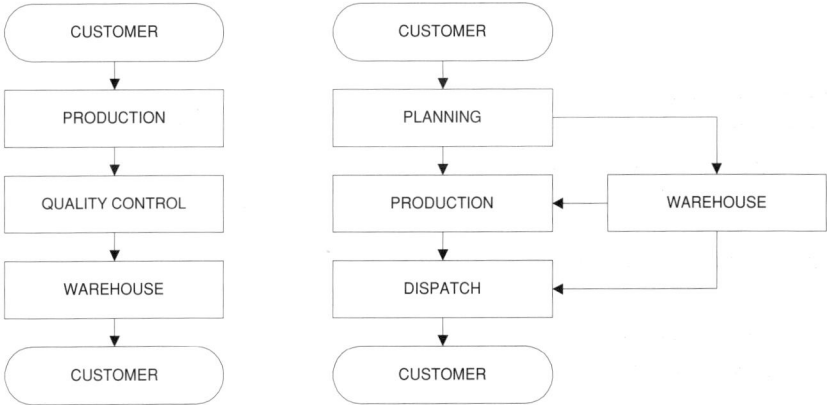

Figure 5.3 Functional relationship   Figure 5.4 Process relationship

Where there are separate departments for production and quality control for example, these should be depicted in terms of the processes executed not the functions that execute them. A functional relationship is illustrated in Figure 5.3 and a process relationship in Figure 5.4 indicating that the inspection and test activities of QC form sub-processes within the production process. When the production process is charted the separate tasks performed by the QC department would be identified.

Don't add every conceivable interconnection at this stage. Only the primary channels should be indicated.

Business process descriptions

On completion of the System Model, a description of each business process should be produced in order to unify understanding and agree a common language. The process descriptions enable functions to determine which tasks are included and which are excluded. The process descriptions should address the following:-

a) The process objective, e.g. The objective of the resource management process is to determine, provide, effectively utilize, maintain and develop the resources required to achieve the organization's objectives.

b) The indicators by which the achievement of the objective will be measured and the method of measurement

c) The process owner (see Chapter 6)

d) Process inputs in terms of the materials and information to be processed

e) Process outputs in terms of the products, services and information delivered

f) The known factors upon which the quality of the process output depends (e.g. skills and competence)

Previously, procedures were established to meet a specific requirement defined by the standard e.g. contract review. However contract review is a task that is part of the sales process the objectives of which are different. The objective of the contract review process is to prevent the organization entering into a commitment with its customers that it is incapable of fulfilling, whereas the objective of the sales process is to secure business for the organization that meets the business objectives.

Previously the success indicators for many parts of the QMS were based on whether the task had been carried out, not whether the objective of the task had been accomplished. Therefore a success indicator for contract review was a tick in a box when it should have been the number of orders accepted that fully met customer expectations.

Summary

The previous approach resulted in a model of the organization centred around the standard that bore little relationship to the way business was conducted (see Table 5.1). A more effective approach has been explained in this chapter that puts the business at the centre and the standard in the role of providing a supporting framework.

This has been shown as achievable by modelling the business as a series of 'end to end' processes. These processes were shown to be those that transform stakeholder needs into satisfaction. This chapter has explained how top management team can derive that common picture of the business and identify the key business processes which need to be in place to deliver the business results

When the common picture or system model has been defined, teams can be formed to develop these business processes as will be explained in the next chapter.

Table 5.1 Contrast between old and new model of the business

Old approach	New approach
Quality manual that paraphrases the standard with little correlation to the business	System description that describes how the business is managed
Procedures that respond to the requirements of the standard	Business processes that achieve business objectives
Functionally based documentation	Process based documentation
Task based procedures	Objective driven processes
Focus on order driven activities	Focus on market and stakeholder driven processes

Chapter 6.

Organizing process development teams

Learning outcomes

After studying this chapter you should be able to:-

❑ understand the difference between the functional approach and the process approach to process development

❑ recognize that people will not instinctively think in terms of a process

❑ recognize that process development is an iterative process which constantly reveals new information about processes

❑ determine the relationships between functions and processes

Change in direction

ISO 9001:1994 required a quality manual and procedures consistent with the requirements of the standard and work instructions defining the manner of production, installation and servicing. This was often interpreted as three levels of documentation. Often an external consultant would write the level 1 quality manual, the quality manager or the consultant would write the 20 or so level 2 procedures and the functional managers would write the level 3 documents - the work instructions. Although there was no requirement for manuals of work instructions for each function, it is how many organization met the requirements. This led to a functional structure of documentation produced by people who, with few exceptions, did not meet with others outside their department in developing the documentation.

ISO 9001:2000 requires documented processes that achieve quality objectives. At the high level, such processes span many functions. It should be clear that each function cannot merely change its manuals of work instructions into manuals of process instructions because this will in itself not define the business processes.

All work is a process and is executed from beginning to end regardless of which department the people come from.

34

Many processes may be common to several departments. With the functional approach there is a tendency towards multiple ways of doing something rather than focusing on best practice for the organization. A change in direction is clearly required.

It is therefore necessary to bring the people together who contribute to a process in order to optimise effectiveness and how this can be accomplished will become apparent from reading this chapter.

Moving from function to process

As stated above, with the 'document what you do' approach organizations often generated departmental manuals of procedures that only involved those within the department. There was often no reflection on why they were doing something as it was assumed that what they did actually generated what was required. There was also little consideration given to the interconnections between departments and their activities and the focus was on departmental conformity rather than on business performance. There was also a focus on departmental objectives often to the detriment of overall business performance. For example purchasing departments often perceived they were meeting business objectives by minimizing their material spend, but in reality, the cheaper materials often caused excessive processing and rework further down stream. This is symptomatic of the functional approach to QMS development. The functional approach structures the QMS around who does what, and not around why things are done nor what they aim to achieve.

The process approach starts with the overall objectives and works backwards, identifying the key activities required to achieve the objectives followed by the identification of skills, competencies and resources. With the process approach, the functions are secondary. The key to effective process development is to involve the people who contribute to the measured outputs. The first step is to identify the activities that deliver the outputs then identify who performs the activities - this is not easy. Because people think functionally they often do not appreciate that they are part of a process that spans many functions. Following identification of the high level business processes (see Chapter 5) the functions that carry out activities that contribute to each process can be identified. When representatives from the functions get together to identify process inputs, tasks, outputs, measures etc, it will become apparent that other functions are involved but not present.

As more people are involved a clearer understanding of the process develops. We can refer to this grouping of people as the Process Development Team.

What may have been thought of as a process confined to a single function, emerges as a process with a multifunctional dimension. It is also likely that as more thought is given to each process and its objectives, new interfaces and process boundaries emerge to make the original system model inadequate and further iteration necessary. It will also be revealed that some activities identified may not contribute effectively to any of the processes. These can be referred to as 'non-value-adding activities' and may be subsequently dispensed with.

An example of this iterative process is the Human Resource Management Process. Initially, the only functions identified may be the HR Department. As they analyze the HR processes, it emerges that many other functions are involved in achieving HR process objectives and by the time the process development team reaches maturity, it may comprise representatives of every function in the organization. From ISO 9001:1994 the only procedure required was for identifying training needs which was very often simply satisfied by creating a training matrix and associated training records. From ISO 9001:2000 there are far wider requirements which can only be satisfied by defining the HR process in its entirety including HR planning, recruitment and selection or contracting, deployment and induction, training, development, welfare and termination. Also included must be the assessment of competence, effectiveness of training and evaluation of performance. There is such a vast difference from the 1994 version of the standard and therefore it is easy to see that the HR process is far more complex and multifunctional than the simplistic approach taken by ISO 9001:1994.

Deploying functions to model

There are a number of ways to establish an effective process development team. A well tried method is to get together the functional heads to produce a Function Matrix which lists all Functional Groups, Departments, Sections etc down the left side and the processes along the top. At the intersections a bullet is placed where the function contributes to the process. The bullet should represent key process actions or decisions taken by the function, not mere presence at a meeting or receipt of information. An example is shown in Table 6.1.

Creation of the Function Matrix is a key stage in identifying who is involved in what and helps involve the right people in the development process who will form a Process Development Team.

If some people are unsure, don't worry as their role in each process will become clear once the process analysis begins. It is common, at this stage for people to realise, often

Table 6.1 Function matrix

Function	Business management	Marketing	Sales	Product /service generation	Order fulfilment	Resource management	Quality system management
Executive Management	●	●				●	●
Marketing		●	●			●	●
Sales		●	●		●	●	●
Design		●	●	●		●	●
Purchasing						●	●
Production Planning				●		●	●
Production				●	●	●	●
Inspection				●	●	●	●
Inventory control				●	●	●	●
Maintenance						●	●
Quality Assurance	●	●	●	●	●	●	●
Dispatch					●		

for the first time, that everything they do is part of a process or processes. The concept of "joined up" is often taken for granted. It is only when the discussion and analysis takes place that the concept becomes reality.

When each function has identified the processes to which it contributes, the identity of the person who will represent the function in a particular process should be determined. The Function Representative should be a person who is knowledgeable about the operations of the function and has authority to act on the group's behalf concerning the description of its practices.

When the representatives have been nominated, the bullets can be replaced with names. A person may represent more than one function if no other suitable person can be nominated. The Matrix then enables the personnel to be identified who will form the Process Development Teams.

Appointing the process owner

When the core business processes have been identified, a Process Owner should be appointed for each business process. The role of the process owner is to drive the process development effort and lead the team of people designing and constructing the processes so that they achieve the prescribed objectives. The process owner is someone who has the skills and competence to facilitate development and keep their eye on the ball. This may not necessarily be a functional manager.

Team development

Each member of the process development team has to undergo process management training in which they understand the fundamental concepts of process management and the differences between the 'document what you do' approach and the 'process' approach. (Getting them to read Chapters 1 & 2 of this book would be a good start) It is useful to start each team meeting with a reminder of process management concepts (see panel) to ensure that the development is kept on course.

Summary

The key to effective process development is to involve the people who contribute to the measured outputs. It is necessary to bring people together so that they can discover the real objectives of a process including who interfaces with whom, when and what passes between them. Process development is an iterative process therefore as more people are involved, a clearer understanding of the process develops. When process development teams have been formed, a more detailed process analysis can commence as will be explained in the next chapter.

Key concepts

- All work is a process.

- All processes serve as a means to achieve objectives.

- Who does what is irrelevant providing they are competent to do it.

- Every process has inputs, outputs constraints and resources.

- Every output must connect with another process and supply some of that process's inputs.

- Every input must arise from the outputs of another process.

- Every input, constraint or resource is supplied by a process.

- Management of a process involves managing the sequence and interaction of events and measuring and monitoring their outputs

---

Chapter 7.

Process analysis

Learning outcomes

After studying this chapter you should be able to:-

❑ describe the key elements of a process

❑ establish performance indicators and measurements for each process

❑ produce process flow charts that link together to form a coherent system description

❑ identify the extent to which the processes meet the requirements of governing standards

❑ identify the changes that need to be made to ensure the processes are effective

❑ select an appropriate type of document for communicating relevant process information

❑ understand the importance of culture on process performance and how to minimise its effects

Change in direction

ISO 9001:1994 required production, installation and servicing processes to be identified but no other processes. It also required these processes be planned and carried out under controlled conditions which were to include documented procedures and the monitoring of process parameters. ISO 9001:2000 takes a completely different approach. It requires the organization to measure, monitor and analyse processes, determine their sequence and interaction and determine criteria and methods to ensure effective operation and control. A process that is operating effectively delivers the required outputs of the required quality, on time, economically while meeting the policies and regulations that apply. This won't happen if left to chance, it has to be engineered - work has to be done to design a process with this understanding of effectiveness in mind.

Previously, all that was in most people's minds was to 'document what you do'. In some cases processes were operating effectively, but what was captured was at best a sequence of activities and at worst, a list of responsibilities. Much of what makes a process effective was left undiscovered, undocumented, not understood and probably not managed. What is required is clearly a change in direction away from documenting what exists to designing effective processes - a task, the complexity of which will become apparent from reading this chapter.

Nature of processes

Processes comprise the actions and decisions required to transform the inputs into outputs which meet process objectives. However there are different types of activities and every activity requires adequate resources, information and a suitable environment for an effective transformation to take place. A popular way to define a process is through a flow chart. However, the flow chart should not be construed as being the process, as it is merely a diagrammatic representation of a process.

To obtain a better understanding of the organization's processes it is necessary to perform a process analysis. Each process has a number of inherent characteristics.

❑ Products or information that is to be processed

❑ Objectives for the performance of the process

❑ Instructions which convey requirements for the product or information to be processed

❑ Planning activities which establish who is to do what, when, how, where and why

❑ Preparatory activities which set-up conditions for commencing work

❑ Result-producing activities that act upon the inputs in the sequence they are executed

❑ Interfaces between activities and other processes supplying resources, product or information

❑ Interfaces between sequential activities receiving or supplying product or information required for processing

❑ Measurement activities for verifying that inputs and outputs meet requirements

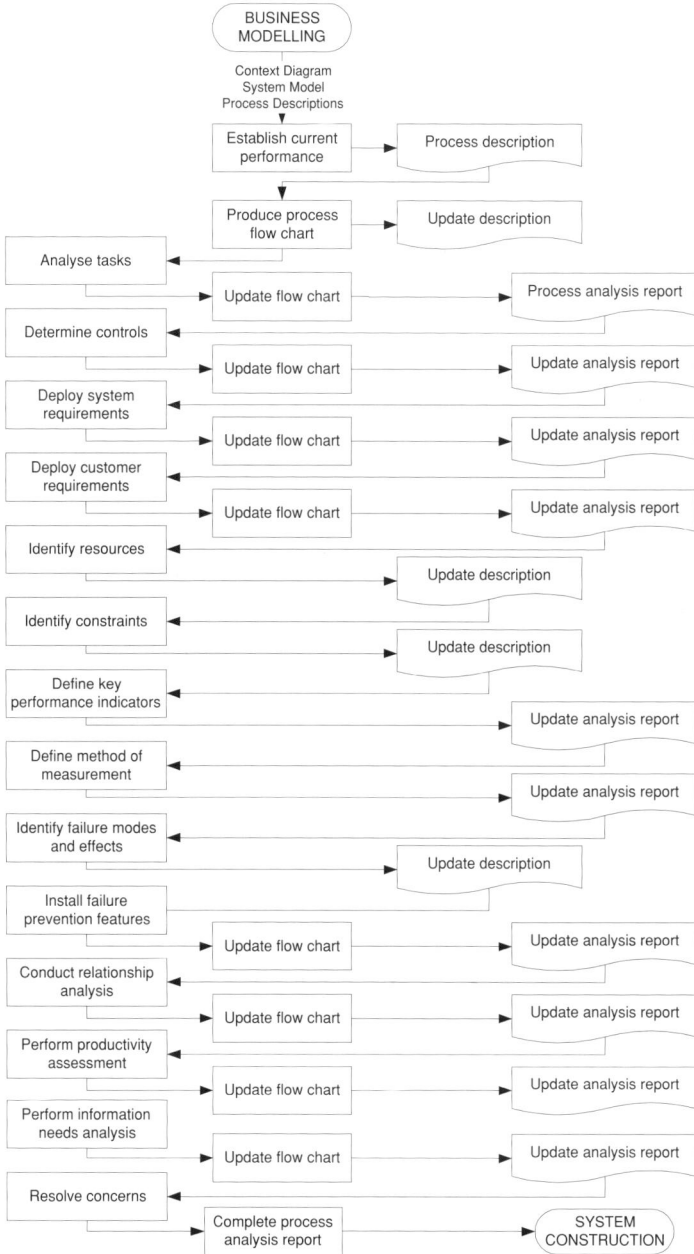

Figure 7.1 Process analysis process

❑ Measurement activities that verify that the process performs as intended

❑ Data collection points that capture data needed to judge process capability

❑ Diagnostic activities that discover the cause of variation

❑ Decision stages where decision makers consider the facts and decide on a course of action

❑ Feedback loops which return product or information for reprocessing

❑ Routing activities which move outputs including waste from one stage to another

❑ Resources which energize the activities and decisions including people, time, materials, machines, facilities, space etc

❑ Constraints which prevent, restrict, limit or regulate events.

The process for carrying out an analysis of processes is illustrated in Figure 7.1 following which each of the stages are described in more detail. Information gathered about the existing processes should be recorded in a Process Description and the results of the analysis in a Process Analysis Report as this will contain the changes to be made.

Key performance indicators (KPIs)

The process objectives were identified in Chapter 4 and having produced a diagrammatic representation of the process it is necessary to determine how achievement of these objectives will be indicated. For example, the objective of a purchasing process might be to supply the organization with the products and services it requires to meet its objectives. As the objectives may cover, financial, societal quality, productivity, innovation aspects, performance indicators for this process might be :-

❑ cost to the business of product/service under and oversupplied (right product, wrong quantity)

❑ cost to the business of releasing defective product/service into the organization (right product, wrong quality)

❑ number of occasions where the wrong product was released into the organization (wrong product)

❑ cost to the business of purchasing from suppliers that fail to sustain delivery performance (right product, right quality, wrong time)

Performance measurement

For each performance indicator it is necessary to determine the method by which performance will be measured. The method will require:-

❑ the data that needs to be collected

❑ where the data is generated

❑ how the data will be collected

❑ how often the data needs to be collected

❑ what analysis needs to be carried out

❑ who is to perform the data collection and analysis

❑ who is to make the decision on whether performance meets target

Current performance assessment

In order to provide the driver for improvement the current performance from the process must be determined. Data should be collected using the agreed performance measures and the gap between desired and current performance determined. This gap gives the "Size of the Prize"

These process measures might be expressed in terms of:-

a) throughput (quantity of information or products that are processed in a given time)

b) time through the process from receipt of inputs to release of outputs

c) process start-up, set-up, shutdown or downtime

d) operating costs

e) satisfaction levels

It is vital to establish a clear linkage between the process objective and performance measures and the achievement of the business objectives.

Process flow charts

On completion of the System model, the descriptions of business processes and the Function Matrix, the Process Development Team can commence development of the process charts. The first series of charts to develop is the business process charts. As each is completed, charts for each work process can be developed. This is an iterative process whereby the business process charts and system model are revisited to modify them as more and more facts emerge.

Some simple charting conventions are shown in Figure 7.2. These are not drawing logic charts or software data flow charts - these represent the sequence of actions and decisions that occur in the process and notes of some key facts about them.

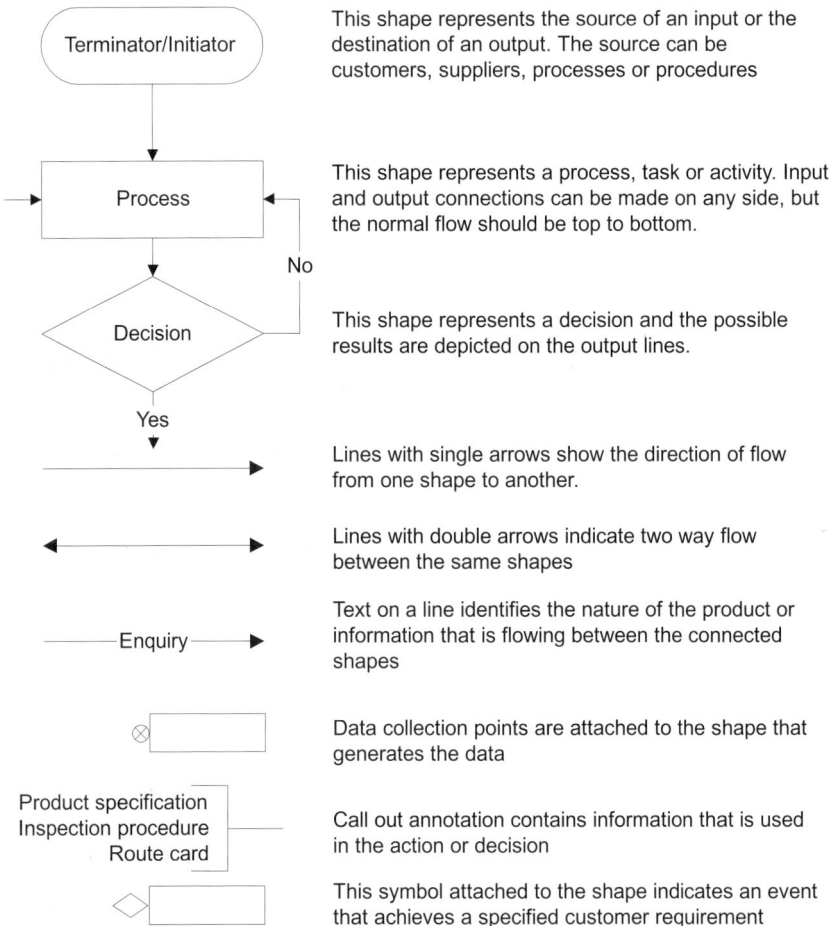

Terminator/Initiator	This shape represents the source of an input or the destination of an output. The source can be customers, suppliers, processes or procedures
Process	This shape represents a process, task or activity. Input and output connections can be made on any side, but the normal flow should be top to bottom.
Decision	This shape represents a decision and the possible results are depicted on the output lines.
	Lines with single arrows show the direction of flow from one shape to another.
	Lines with double arrows indicate two way flow between the same shapes
Enquiry	Text on a line identifies the nature of the product or information that is flowing between the connected shapes
	Data collection points are attached to the shape that generates the data
Product specification Inspection procedure Route card	Call out annotation contains information that is used in the action or decision
	This symbol attached to the shape indicates an event that achieves a specified customer requirement

Figure 7.2 Charting conventions

Taking the inputs and outputs defined in the system model, describe each business process in flow chart form. Draw the process flow chart showing:-

a)   Interfaces with other processes (where inputs come from and outputs go to)

b)   Interfaces with external organizations

c)   Sequence of tasks (what happens next)

d)   Responsibilities (who does what)

e)   Documentation used

f)   Data recording points

g)   Data collection points (data for measuring and deciding process/product performance)

h)   Routing of collected data for analysis

i)   The stages where specified customer requirements are achieved.

The chart should reflect how business is currently conducted, not how people think it is conducted or how it should be conducted. An example is shown in Figure 7.3.

Although, it is not the purpose of quality system development to merely document what you do now it is necessary to commence with an accurate description of processes as they currently exist. Chart the sequence of events that follow receipt of the input from the feeding processes to the output that is transmitted to the receiving processes.

If the input or output interface is with an external organization the chart will either start or end with a link to that organization. All work requires an input to commence. In many cases the input is either a product or a piece of information. Even with time dependent tasks, the task commences with the release of the time schedule that stipulates when the task is to be performed. Ask the question "Where do the instructions come from to trigger this process?" The decomposition of the system is illustrated in Figure 7.4 The sub-system category is only necessary when a business process consists of several major processes. Product/service generation and resource management are examples where an intermediate division of processes is needed in order to capture different versions of the same generic process.

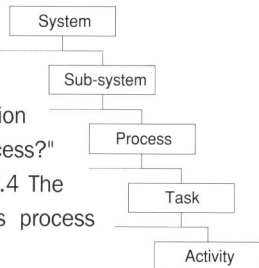

Figure 7.4 System decomposition

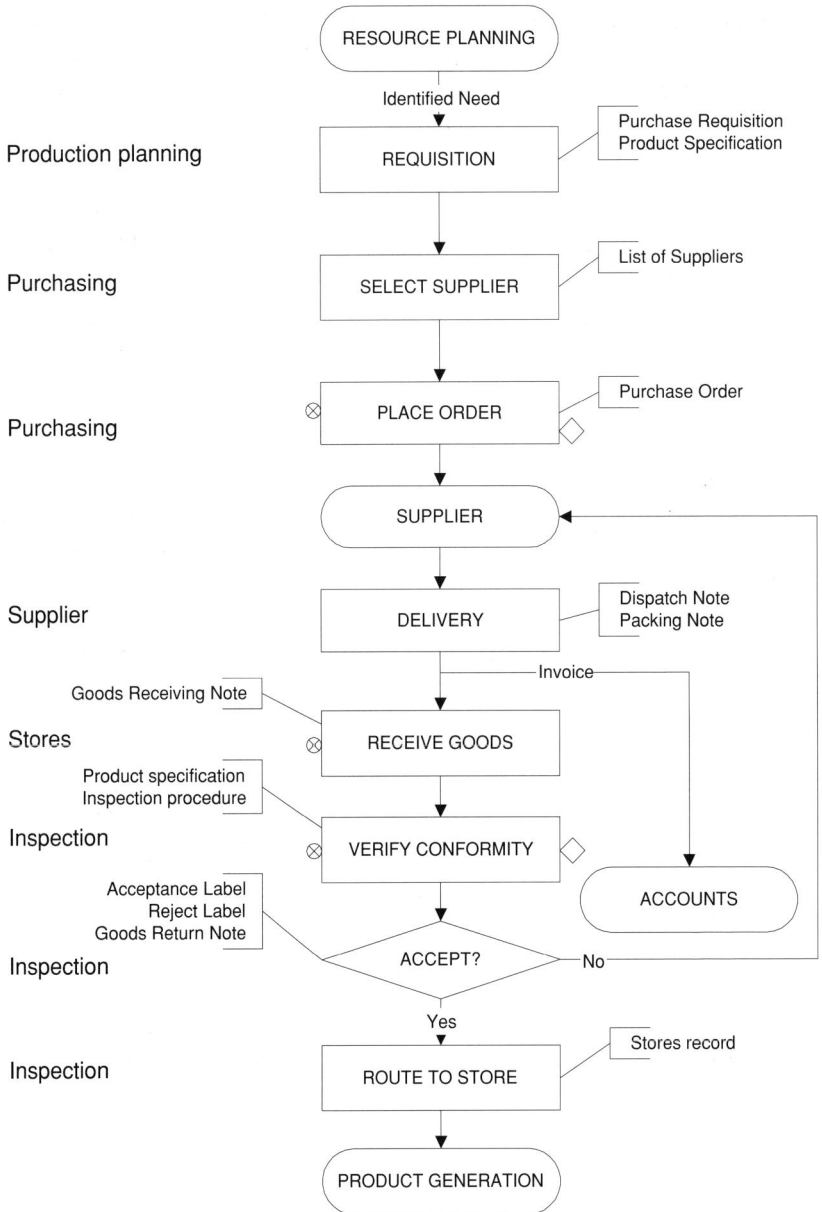

Figure 7.3 Sample process flow chart

The decomposition of processes is illustrated in Figure 7.5. Here we take one of the business processes of the system model, identify the tasks that constitute the business process and form the second tier of flow charts. Next we take each task of a business process and identify the activities that constitute the work processes to form further flow charts.

The inputs and outputs should be shown at each stage in the decomposition. This illustration is symbolic, the tasks may interface with other processes and there may be decision tasks as well as action tasks.

The tasks in the business process chart are likely to cross functional boundaries so that the responsibility for each task is different. At the work process level, the responsibility for each activity may be the same but it may take several tiers before reaching this level.

So that the suite of charts reflects a coherent system, it is important to ensure all process linkages are in place. Ensure all process initiators and terminators link to other processes, or in the case of business inputs and outputs, ensure they link to the external organizations. Also ensure the titles used in the initiators and terminators are

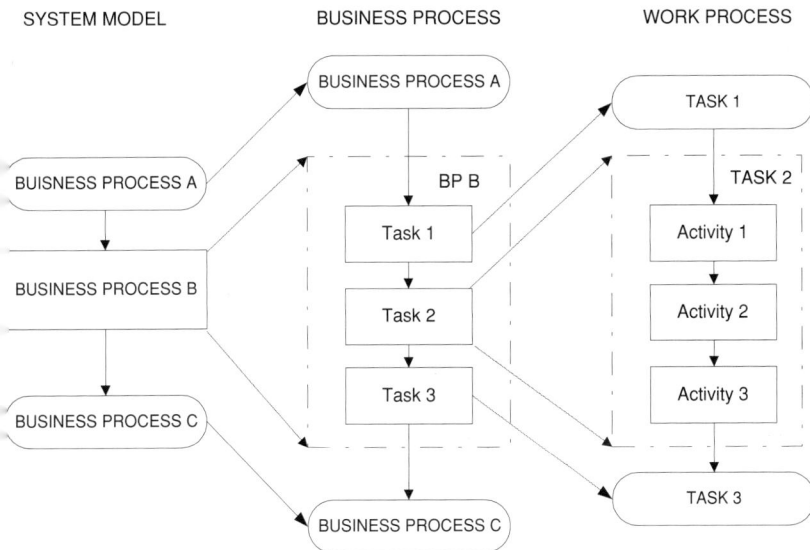

gure 7 5 Process decomposition

the same as the processes feeding the inputs or receiving the outputs.

Task analysis

Often what is known about a task is that which is described in the related procedures. If these have been produced using ISO 9001:1994 or ISO 9002:1994 as the guide, many aspects essential for its effective operation may have been overlooked. The task itself may also not fulfil a useful purpose within the process.

For each task in the flow chart ask:

❑ Is the objective of the task clearly understood?

❑ Does the task provide an output which serves the process objective?

❑ Do we have measures for its performance?

❑ Have we got an effective method of measuring performance?

❑ Do we have results that indicate that the task is performing to target?

❑ Is the output provided at the appropriate stage in the process?

❑ Is this the only process that generates this output?

If the answer to any of these is 'no' the issue needs to be resolved before proceeding further.

It is also useful to perform a comprehensive task analysis in order to discover the characteristics upon which its effectiveness depends. Such an analysis will reveal the current basis for performing the task as well as any omissions. A useful technique is to analyze each task on the flow chart by applying *Kipling's Law* which states:

"I keep six honest serving-men

They taught me all I know;

Their names are What and Why and When

And How and Where and Who."

(*Rudyard Kipling*).

Table 7.1 illustrates how this can be put into practice to obtained information that uniquely characterises each task. The results may be used as inputs into a Process Description or displayed on the relevant process charts.

Table 7.1 Task analysis questionnaire

Inputs	• What are the inputs? • Why are they supplied? • Where do they come from? • Who supplies them? • How are they supplied? • When are they supplied?	• How are they measured? • What happens if inputs are incorrect? • What source traceability is required? • How frequently are they supplied? • How are they held pending use? • What happens if they are late?
Resources	• What resources are required? • Why are they needed? • Where do they come from? • Who supplies them? • How are they supplied? • When are they supplied?	• What skills and tools are required? • What information is required? • How frequently are they required? • How are they measured? • What happens if they are incorrect? • What source traceability is required?
Task	• What is performed? • Why is it performed? • Where is it performed? • Who performs it? • How is it performed? • When is it performed?	• What is the preceding step? • What approvals are needed to start? • What precautions need to be observed? • How is performance measured? • What happens when failure is encountered? • What happens if the task is omitted?
Constraints	• What are the constraints? • Why are the constraints necessary? • Where in this process are they applied? • Who imposes the constraints? • How are they addressed? • When do they apply?	• What effect do they have on performance? • Who checks that the constraints are maintained? • What happens if they are not maintained? • How frequently are the checks performed? • What is at risk if constraints are removed? • How would their removal be detected?
Outputs	• What are the outputs? • Why are they needed? • Where do they go to? • Who receives them? • How are they supplied? • When are they supplied?	• How are they measured? • What happens if they are not correct? • What source traceability is required? • What happens if they are late? • How is waste dealt with? • What happens next?

Control analysis

Once the initial chart has been developed a control analysis should be performed to identify key controls. Using the generic process model in Figure 7.6, examine the initial process charts to identify the following:

a)   What constitutes the input requirement and how is this measured?

b)   What constitutes the planning or preparation tasks? (i.e. What has to be in place to start the process correctly?)

c)   What constitutes the doing tasks? (i.e. What has to be done to produce the correct outputs?)

d)   What constitutes the checking tasks before release of process output? (i.e. When and how are the outputs measured?)

e)   What constitutes the remedial action tasks in the event that the checking tasks reveal problems?

f)   What constitutes the corrective action tasks?

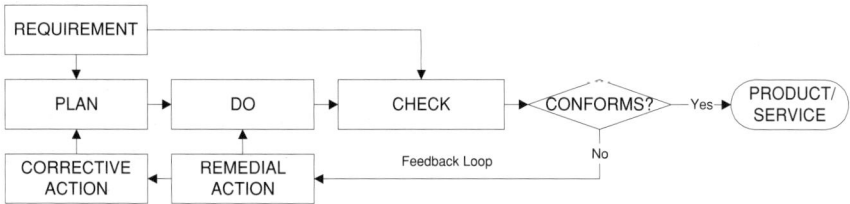

Figure 7.6 Generic control process

If a) to f) above cannot be satisfied and the equivalent tasks identified in the process chart, add tasks or redefine tasks to indicate both product and process controls.

The inputs should be shown on the input feed lines and outputs on the output feed lines. The interfaces between processes should be matched with one another so that the charts represent the flow of work through a process and the complete suite of charts reflects a coherent system with no gaps, overlaps, dead ends or loose ends.

System requirement deployment

An approach taken to ISO 9000 by many organizations was to respond to the requirements of the standard in the sequence they were stated. This approach assumed that the requirements were firstly listed in a logical order and secondly that the requirements covered every process the organization needed to employ.

The requirements of ISO 9001:1994 were those considered necessary to provide an adequate assurance of product quality and not those provisions that were necessary to market, design, procure, produce, supply and maintain products that meet satisfy customers. There are therefore activities that were not addressed by the standard.

A more appropriate approach is to model the business as described in chapter 5 and then deploy or map the requirements onto the identified processes. In this way any gaps will be identified where the processes would be noncompliant.

After creating the system model, associated business processes and work process charts, the requirements of the external standards and regulations should be deployed onto the flow charts and a series of Compliance Matrices of the form in Table 7.2 produced. An even more robust approach is to use ISO 9004 in the matrix thereby identifying opportunities for improvement beyond mere compliance with ISO 9001:2000.

Where requirements of the standard cannot be matched with any task or decision in the suite of charts, a gap may have been identified. In principle, a requirement of an external standard (e.g. ISO 9001, TS/ISO 16949, QS-9000) or regulation (e.g. Environmental Pollution Act) would only result in a new task or activity on a process chart if the requirement related to a task or activity not currently carried out in the organization.

Customer requirement deployment

Process stages where specific customer needs and expectations are satisfied should be identified and annotated the charts with the designated symbol (see Figure 7.2).

Table 7.2 Compliance matrix

ISO 9001:2000 Clause	Business management	Marketing	Sales	Product/ service generation	Order fulfilment	Resource management	Quality System Management
4.1							●
4.2							●
5.1	●						
5.2	●						
5.3	●						
5.4.1	●						
5.4.2	●						
5.5.1	No requirements						
5.5.2	●						
5.5.3	●						
5.5.4							●
5.5.5							●
5.5.6							●
5.5.7							●
5.6.1							●
5.6.2							●
5.6.3							●
6.1						●	
6.2.1						●	
6.2.2						●	
6.3						●	
6.4						●	
7.1					●		
7.2.1		●					
7.2.2			●				
7.2.3		●	●				●
7.3.1				●			
7.3.2				●			
7.3.3				●			
7.3.4				●			
7.3.5				●			
7.3.6				●			
7.3.7				●			
7.4.1						●	●
etc							

Failure modes and effects

A powerful but under utilized method of improving the effectiveness and performance of processes is Failure Modes and Effects Analysis (FMEA). A failure modes and effects analysis is a systematic analytical technique for identifying potential failures in the design of a product or process, assessing the probability of occurrence and likely effect and determining the measures needed to eliminate, contain or control the effects.

Firstly each function of the process is identified i.e. the outcomes the process is designed to accomplish. For each outcome it is necessary to establish the:-

a) Potential failure modes (the manner in which the process could potentially fail to meet the design intent)

b) Potential effects of failure in terms of what the customer of the output might notice or experience.

c) Severity of the effect (a numerical range of 1 to 10, can be used to grade severity with 10 being hazardous without warning and 1 having no effect)

d) Classification of the effect in terms of whether it is critical, key, major or significant

e) Potential cause(s)/mechanism(s) of failure

f) Occurrence (the likelihood that a specific cause/mechanism will occur - a numerical range of 1 to 10 can be used for probability of occurrence with 10 being almost inevitable and 1 being unlikely)

g) Current design/process controls in terms of the prevention, verification or other activities to assure process adequacy

h) Probability of detection (a numerical range of 1 to 10 can be used for detection probability with 10 meaning that the control will not detect the potential failure and 1 meaning that the control will almost certainly detect the potential cause of failure)

f) Risk priority number (this is the number 1-1000 generated from multiplying the severity, occurrence and detection factors. This element is not essential but does make the result numerical and hence comparable. The higher the result the higher priority needs to be given to it).

Failure prevention features

For each process failure mode ensure that provisions are in place to eliminate, control or reduce the effects of failure. Determine the changes required to make the process robust and update the FMEA in order to show:-

❑ Recommended actions, prioritising action on the highest ranked concerns

❑ Responsibility for actions

❑ Actions taken

❑ Resulting severity, occurrence, detection ranking and risk priority number. This is computed after the actions have been taken so as to indicate the degree of improvement.

Relationship analysis

From the function descriptions and flow charts, relationships should be assessed for conflict of responsibility and authority. These may manifest themselves by:-

❑ duplication of activities and decisions such as checking work more than once, repeating work of other groups etc

❑ decisions taken by personnel other than those responsible for the work

❑ frequent transfer of product or information between groups within a process

Where such instances appear unjustified, establish the cause and propose arrangements to simplify the process.

Productivity assessment

Actual information flow should be assessed to identify the number of transactions caused by inputs or outputs not being complete before work commences.

The frequency that work recycles the feedback loops should also be assessed to identify ineffective practices.

In developing the ISO 9001:1994 system many more checks, inspections and reviewing points than are actually necessary may have been introduced. Assess decision points and establish whether they are justified in terms of their impact on process objectives and are being taken neither too soon, too frequently, nor too late to detect failure.

Information needs analysis

The task analysis will produce a great deal of information about the process and it is necessary to determine what information will be needed for the effective and efficient operation and control of the process. ISO 9000:2000 defines a document as *information and its support medium.* Therefore documents are carriers of information. From the task analysis several pieces of information will have been identified - information that defines or conveys:

❑ inputs

❑ work requirements

❑ verification requirements

❑ movement requirements

❑ methods

❑ reference data

❑ guidance material

❑ records

❑ identity

❑ outputs

If the information is not required to operate and control the process effectively and efficiently, it cannot be essential and therefore serious consideration should be given to whether it needs to be documented and maintained. The 'document what you do approach' led to a proliferation of procedures and records without a need necessarily being established, other than a perceived requirement within ISO 9000. The needs for documentation should be derived from the needs of the process. From the task analysis a list of information needs can be generated. Having obtained an answer to each question in the task analysis, establish the form in which the information will be conveyed to, within and from the process. A range of information carriers is defined in Table 7.3.

Cultural analysis

Culture is the values, beliefs and norms that permeate an organization and help to shape the behaviour of its members. Culture guides an organization in meeting its objectives, in working with one another and in dealing with the stakeholders. As processes serve to achieve objectives it follows that culture is a key factor in the effectiveness of business processes. A cultural analysis is therefore necessary to establish those aspects of behaviour that impact process performance.

There will be cultural factors that are affecting the current performance of a process. Some of these may be advantageous and some detrimental. In moving to a process approach, some beliefs will have to change. The cultural traits that act as drivers and barriers to system effectiveness need to be identified so that the impact of change is

Table 7.3 Information carriers

Information carrier	Purpose
Policies	Policies are used to define constraints over actions and decisions so that they meet the needs of stakeholders.
Control procedures	Control procedures control work on a product or information as it passes through a process.
Operating procedures	Operating procedures prescribe how specific tasks are to be performed.
Standards	Standards define acceptance criteria for judging the quality of an activity, a document, a result, a product or a service.
Guides	Guides aid decision making and conduct of activities.
Blank forms	Blank forms are used to collect and transmit information for analysis or approval.
Blank labels	Labels identify product status and are often disposed of when the status changes.
Notices	Notices alert staff to regulations that must be followed, to precautions and to dangers that exist.
Job descriptions	Job descriptions define the responsibility, authority and accountability of personnel.
Specifications	Specifications are used to define requirements for a task, a product, a service or a process.
Plans	Plans are used to define provisions made to achieve objectives.
Reports	Reports are used to convey the results of an activity.
Instructions	Instructions are used to define specific tasks that are required.
Records	Records are used to capture information that is needed for subsequent analysis, decision-making or demonstration.

fully recognized and accepted by management before proceeding beyond system design.

Any installation requires a firm foundation and the purpose of analysis to establish what changes have to be made to prepare the foundations for a successful installation. Some of these will pervade all processes and some may be process-specific and not become apparent until much later. What is important at this stage is to identify the key cultural changes that need to pervade the whole organization.

Resolving concerns

Identify unknowns, conflicts, or differences in approach and resolve with those concerned. Deal with concerns promptly as they may signal more serious problems that will plague the conversion.

System design documentation

The results of system design should be contained in a process analysis report, a system description and several process descriptions.

Process analysis reports

The Process Analysis Reports should be completed by including the results of all the process analysis activities performed with recommendations as to changes that need to be made. Separate reports may be desirable for business and work processes. (The content is outlined in Chapter 9).

System description

A system description is a document that contains the high level information about the QMS. Its life begins following agreement of the Systems Requirements and provides a vehicle for containing the results of the business modelling. It may be consolidated with the process descriptions to form a manual that would have all the characteristics of a Quality Manual and be a lot more useful. The system description can perform a vital role in demonstrating that the system has been well designed to achieve the business objectives. In effect it describes the way the business is managed and hence it is useful for new people, for training and for staff development as well as for satisfying the requirements of ISO 9001:2000. The contents of a typical system description are itemised in Chapter 9.

Process descriptions

A Process Description is a document that contains or references everything known about a process. During process analysis, information is collected describing the current process. Following implementation of the recommendations in the Process Analysis Report, the Process Description is updated to reflect the modified process. Process Descriptions may be maintained for both business and work processes as discrete documents or combined into a manual. The content of a typical process description is outlined in Chapter 9.

Process development plan

As existing documentation is matched to needs and new processes, tasks and activities are identified a Process Development Plan should be produced that defines the activities necessary to implement the recommendations from the process analysis. The content of a typical process development plan is outlined in Chapter 9.

Summary

In this chapter process analysis has been explained as a number of related tasks performed once the system model has been created and the process development teams formed. The sequence and interaction of tasks and processes is only one element of process analysis, albeit a major part and this results in process flow charts but process analysis does not end there.

ISO 9001:2000 requires processes to be identified, their sequence and interaction determined, criteria and methods for their effective operation and control determined and the processes measured, monitored and analysed. Hence, flow charts are but one aspect of meeting this requirement. If we analyse these requirements in terms of how they have been addressed so far, the results are as shown in Table 7.4.

This chapter has explained process analysis, sufficient for the reader to identify the major changes that need to be made in order to convert an existing QMS.

The next chapter explains how to put the system design into practice.

Table 7.4 How the book addresses the requirements of ISO 9001:2000

Requirement	Addressed by	Chapter
Processes identified	Modelling the business	4
	Process flow charting	6
Process sequence and interaction	System model	4
	Process charts	6
Criteria and methods for effective operation and control	Task analysis	6
	Control analysis	6
	Failure modes and effects analysis	6
	Productivity assessment	6
	Relationship analysis	6
	System requirement deployment	6
	Customer requirement deployment	6
Measure, monitor and analyse processes	Key performance indicators	6
	Current performance assessment	6
	Data recording and collection points	6
	Routing of collected data for analysis	6

Chapter 8.

System construction

Learning outcomes

After studying this chapter you should be able to:-

❑ understand the steps to be taken to construct a system that fulfils the design criteria

❑ understand why documentation is needed, what needs to be documented and how these needs differ depending on risks

❑ install and commission new processes and change existing processes

❑ understand the importance of behaviour in making process effective

Change in direction

ISO 9001:1994 required the system to be documented and the documents to be reviewed and approved prior to issue. ISO 9001:2000 still requires the system to be documented and documents to be approved prior to issue, but the important change arises from the requirement for the processes to be managed. Process management is not simply about managing documents - documents are required but as a means for capturing and conveying information about the processes and their outputs. In order to manage a process one needs to manage all the inherent characteristics of the process in such a manner that the requirements of customers and interested parties are fulfilled by its outputs. This means managing information, resources, behaviour and results. Management of processes starts when they are being designed and continues through their construction into operations and maintenance and further into their evaluation and continuous improvement. Hence, ISO 9001:2000 introduces a different perspective on system documentation and implementation and presents a significant change in direction as will become apparent from reading this chapter.

Process development

Each business process should proceed through development as defined in the process development plan. At the end of process analysis the components of each process will have been identified to a level where process development can commence. This will invariably involve the following tasks:-

❑ Producing or revising documentation

❑ Maintaining a register of documents

❑ Refining the business process flow charts

❑ Procuring additional resources

❑ Redefining people's responsibilities and authority

❑ Designing/selecting data capture tools

❑ Designing/selecting data analysis tools

The output of process development will be a set of documents that describe each of the business process and work processes to a level necessary to ensure repeatable performance providing the people have:-

❑ the ability to do the job

❑ the motivation to do the job

❑ the resources to do the job

Providing this environment is the subject of process and system integration.

Reasons for documenting information

The degree of documentation varies from a simple statement of fact to details of how a specific activity is to be carried out. To document everything you do would be impractical and of little value. There are however, several good reasons for documenting information:-

❑ To convey requirements and instructions effectively

❑ To convert solved problems into recorded knowledge so as to avoid having to solve them repeatedly

❑ To provide freedom for management and staff to maximise their contribution to the business

- ❑ To free the business from reliance on particular individuals for its effectiveness
- ❑ To provide legitimacy and authority for the actions and decisions needed
- ❑ To make responsibility clear and to create the conditions of self-control
- ❑ To provide co-ordination for inter-departmental action
- ❑ To improve communication and to provide consistency and predictability in carrying out repetitive tasks
- ❑ To provide training and reference material for new and existing staff
- ❑ To provide evidence to those concerned of your intentions and your actions
- ❑ To provide a basis for studying existing work practices and identifying opportunities for improvement
- ❑ To demonstrate after an incident the precautions which were taken or which should have been taken to prevent it or minimise its occurrence

Reasons for not documenting information

There are also several reasons for not documenting information.

- ❑ If the course of action or sequence of steps cannot be predicted a procedure or plan cannot be written for unforeseen events.
- ❑ If there is no effect on performance by allowing freedom of action or decision, there is no mandate to prescribe the methods to be employed.
- ❑ If it cannot be foreseen that any person might need to take action or make a decision using information from a process, there is no mandate to require the results to be recorded.
- ❑ If the action or decision is intuitive or spontaneous, no manner of documentation will ensure a better performance.
- ❑ If the action or decision needs to be habitual, documentation will be beneficial only in enabling the individual reach a level of competence.

Size doesn't matter

Size and type of organization are often thought to influence the degree of documentation needed. However a large organization could be large because of the quantity of assets - 2000 offices with 2 people in each. Or it could be large because it employs 6,000 people, 5,500 of whom do the same job. Size in itself therefore, is not a factor and size without some units of measure is meaningless. Likewise the type of organization will affect what information needs to be recorded but again not the amount of information needed.

Complexity

Complexity is the primary influence on the degree of documentation needed. Complexity is a function of the number of processes and their interconnections in an organization. The more processes, the greater the number of documents. The more interconnections, the greater the detail within those documents. Complexity is also a function of the relationships. The greater the number of relationships, the greater the complexity and channels of communication. Many documents exist simply to communicate information reliably and act as a point of reference should our memory fail us. In the simplest of processes, all the influencing facts can be remembered accurately. As complexity increases, it becomes more difficult to remember all the facts and recall them accurately.

Competency

Competency is a collection of skills, behaviours, attributes and qualifications required to carry out a job. When personnel are new to a job, they need education and training. Documentation is needed to assist in this process for two reasons. Firstly to make the process repeatable and predictable and secondly to provide a memory bank that is more reliable than the human memory. As people learn the job they begin to rely less and less on documentation to the extent that eventually no prescriptive documentation may be used at all to produce the required output.

Competence is the ability to demonstrate use of the skills, behaviours, attributes and qualifications to achieve the result required for the job. Hence competency may depend upon the availability of documentation - knowing where to locate data essential for setting up a machine, or contacting a customer, or processing an invoice. If the documentation cannot be found, the person is unable to do the job and hence cannot demonstrate competence.

Analysing existing documentation

Once the needs have been identified, the existing information relating to each process can be captured. The Development Teams should analyze the information and match existing information to the need in the process description taking into account the linking provisions.

Linking documents

All documents should have a parent document which invokes its use or creation, therefore a hierarchy of documents should be created which results in there being no document in existence in the organization that is not linked to another in the hierarchy. The principle is illustrated in Figure 8.1. If a document cannot be attributed to a process directly, or through a linked document, there will be no trigger to cause the information to be used. If it is believed that the information would be used without such a trigger from the flow chart, the chart must be incomplete and should be revisited until a need has been proven and linked to the process.

Process installation overview

Process installation is concerned with bringing information, human resources and physical resources together in the right relationship so that all the components are put in place in readiness to commence operation. In many cases process installation will require a cultural change. There is little point is introducing change to people who are not prepared for it. Installing a dynamic process based system into an environment in which people still believe in an element based system is doomed to fail. Any installation requires a firm foundation. The cultural analysis will have identified the key changes. Now is the stage during which these changes need to be made.

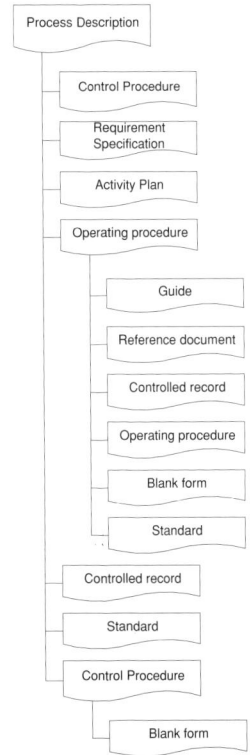

Figure 8.1 Document tree

Preparing the foundations

Top management

To prepare the foundations for a fundamental change in the way the QMS is perceived and managed, the starting point has to be the reorientation of top management. One way of accomplishing this is to get them together and facilitate them to think through the way they operate.

By identifying all the different situations that may arise in a typical business year, get them to assess whether they handle these situations using a functional approach or a process approach. It is not uncommon to find that top management activities feature very few times in the process charts. All the action is at the lower levels. If top management activities are not included in the process flow charts, the processes which achieve the business objectives have not been fully captured.

Staff reorientation

The process development teams should comprise representatives from each contributing function. However, these representatives need to be more than analysts. They need to be the primary means by which staff learn of the changes and the impact they have upon them. General awareness sessions can help but on-the-job instruction is still the best way of making people realize what is involved. Each member of staff will have different perceptions about the organization, its vision, values and processes. Some will be led by others, some will lead the way and some will stand their ground and resist change. Work with the leaders first - they will set examples for others to follow. Leave the diehards until last and you may find they come around when they see they stand out in a crowd.

Testing the foundations

In order to test the foundations use the tables provided in the summaries to each Chapter. Alternatively devise another series of typical situations that characterise the difference between the functional approach and the process approach. As process installation and commissioning takes place, the change in perception can be tested.

Decommissioning the old processes

In some cases new processes can be run alongside old processes but that won't be possible for information-driven processes. Information processes can be terminated while leaving the information dormant in its storage medium. The only change is that people will turn to using new sources of information. It is also wise to retain old software until there is confidence in the new system after which it can safely be removed. A more difficult area to decommission is the informal practice. Few knew it existed and even fewer realized it was essential for process continuity. Those that have been formalized present few problems but those that have been discontinued do present difficulties and are analogous to breaking a habit. Even when the person is aware of the consequences, the habit persists hence vigilance is necessary until the habit has been eradicated.

Another problem is communication. Some organizations thrived upon communication up and down the hierarchy. Under process management, communication has to be primarily lateral through the process and across departmental boundaries. The extent to which this is a barrier will depend on the prevailing management style and could take a long time to change. Again it pays to be vigilant and encourage people to think twice before communicating upwards and ask themselves whether the communication would be more effective if made between the defined stages in the process.

Installing the new processes

The business does not stop while new or modified processes are installed. Installation therefore rarely happens in virgin territory - there are processes operating and delivering results all the time. System installation is therefore a process carried out in measured steps. In many cases there will be minor modifications to processes such as the introduction of new data recording, collection and analysis routines to measure process performance. In other cases there will be new processes to install, such as customer satisfaction measurement. Whatever the case, it is necessary to plan the installation in order to ensure the right people are equipped with the right information and tools to do the right job at the right time.

Armed with the process description, call those concerned together and walk through the process. Gain understanding and commitment and secure the resources to make it happen. This act alone may reveal some things that need to be changed in the process construction but it better to find out at the start than later. Installation means also setting up work areas, equipment, new software and databases, communication tools and other aspects of the process. When the physical aspects have been prepared and everyone involved understands their roles, their responsibilities and how they are to act and react, the process is ready for commissioning.

Process commissioning

Process commissioning is concerned with getting all the new processes working following installation. The people will have been through reorientation and will have received all the necessary process information.

Any new resources will have been acquired and deployed and the old processes decommissioned. Installation and commissioning of new processes takes place sequentially usually without a break so that current operations are not adversely affected.

During commissioning the following activities will be necessary:-

❑   Coaching staff in the new practices and testing understanding

❑   Testing process flow, interfaces and feedback loops

❑   Testing process controls, output quality, delivery and cost

❑   Loading databases with process data

❑   Testing data retrieval and analysis tools

❑   Testing information transfer channels

❑   Testing data analysis and reporting mechanisms

❑   Testing process improvement mechanisms

❑   Testing process robustness, capability and integrity

The old approach was to issue the procedures then walk away. In effectively managed processes, people are led into the job, coached, trained and not left unsupervised until both the process owner and the process operator are satisfied that the desired results are being achieved.

Process integration

Process integration is concerned with changing behaviour so that people do the right things right without having to be told. The hand-holding of the commissioning stage can cease. When process integration is complete, the steps within a process become routine, habits are formed and beliefs strengthened. The way people act and react to certain stimuli becomes predictable and produces results that are required. Improvement does not come about by implementing requirements - it comes about by integrating principles into behaviour.

It may take a long time for integration to occur. Habits may not be formed overnight. People need time to practice and while they are practising they need to be observed so as to alert the process owners to behaviours that need addressing. One way of measuring process integration is through audit. However, the auditor is not only concerned with conformity. The auditor should be looking for actions and reactions to detect whether they reflect the new cultural traits.

Processes operate independently of departmental boundaries and it is at the interface between departments that the greatest problems will arise. The departmental silos protect feudal practices which need to be broken down if the process is to be effective.

System integration

As each process is installed and commissioned the interconnections begin to form into a system. The system will not be effective if the process linkages do not function properly.

❑   One process may operate effectively only by causing an interfacing process to run inefficiently.

❑   The capacity of one process may become a constraint on the whole system.

❑   Restrictive practices in one area may cause bottlenecks elsewhere.

❑   The rate of information output from one process may cause overload on the receiving process.

These and many other problems may arise and until all processes work together in harmony and deliver the desired business outputs, the system is not operating effectively. System integration will take considerably longer to accomplish than the three months usually allocated between issuing procedures and the certification audit. System integration has been an option up until now and no auditors have even attempted to delve into the depths of culture and measuring system effectiveness, so a different approach will have to be taken.

Summary

A number of key messages were contained in this chapter.

❑   ISO 9001:1994 required systems to be documented and implemented - ISO 9001:2000 requires processes to be managed and this is where there is a significant change in direction.

❑ Process management is about managing information, resources, behaviour and results.

❑ Processes will only be effective if people have the ability, resources and motivation to do the job.

❑ All documents are derived from a process need.

❑ The need for documentation is based on process complexity and personnel competency.

❑ All documentation should be linked within the process hierarchy.

❑ Any installation requires a firm foundation - there is little point in introducing change to people who are not prepared for it.

❑ If top management activities are not included in the process flow charts, the processes may not be fully captured.

❑ Informal processes are habits that are difficult to break.

❑ In effectively managed processes, people are led into the job, coached, trained and not left unsupervised - managers don't issue instructions and simply walk away.

❑ The system is not in place until people do the right things right without having to be told and this requires its integration into the fabric of the organization.

Chapter 9.

Conversion complete?

Learning outcomes

After studying this chapter you should be able to:-

❑ determine whether in fact the conversion has been successful

❑ identify where further improvement is required

Process reviews

As with all successful change processes, there is an ongoing need to monitor the conversion process and review the progress made in achieving the defined objectives.

In order to monitor achievements it is necessary to set up a mechanism for process reviews.

Timing

At any point in time after commencing the conversion process, set up a review that establishes the status of the system deliverables.

System deliverables

The conversion process generates a number of deliverables that are indicative of the maturity of the conversion. These deliverables include:-

❑ System description containing:-

- Statement of system purpose and scope
- Statement of system scope
- Business objectives
- System design criteria
- Context diagram
- System model
- Function matrix

- System performance indicators
- System performance measurement method
- System performance results

❑ Process descriptions containing:-

- Process objectives
- Process owner
- Process inputs and outputs
- Process flow charts
- Dependencies (skills, competencies, capabilities)
- Key performance indicators
- Performance measurement methods
- Process performance results

❑ Process Analysis Report containing:-

- Current performance metrics
- Task analysis results
- Control analysis results
- System requirements compliance matrix
- Customer requirements compliance matrix
- Resource analysis results
- Process constraints
- FMEA results
- Relationship analysis results
- Productivity assessment results
- Cultural analysis results
- Open concerns

❑ Process Development Plan containing:-

- New resources to be acquired (space, people, plant)
- New measuring and monitoring equipment/techniques to be installed
- Documentation to be produced (information carriers)
- The target dates for each action
- The responsibilities for each action
- The resources necessary to execute the action
- The outcome from each action
- The manner in which changes to the process will be implemented to overcome resistance to change
- The provisions for removing existing controls

❑ Process development

❑ Process installation

❑ Process commissioning

❑ Process integration

Review criteria

Key aspects to be addressed include:

1) Have the key processes necessary to deliver the business objectives been identified?

2) Do the key processes accurately reflect how product and information is controlled as it passes between the various parts of the business?

3) Are the definitions and outputs of the processes consistent with the business objectives?

4) Have all external and internal interfaces been accounted for?

5) Do the models show that the controls are compliant with the governing standards?

6) Are the models consistent and coherent?

7) Have processes been put in place for determining:-

   a) Stakeholder expectations
   b) Stakeholder satisfaction
   c) System effectiveness

8) Have processes been put in place for managing:-

   a) Supplier relationships?
   b) The QMS?
   c) Business information?
   d) Recruitment, selection and development of human resources including competence definition and assessment?
   e) Physical resources including plant, machinery and facilities?
   f) The human and physical work environment?
   g) Improvement programmes?

9) Would the processes, if implemented as described, enable us to achieve our business objectives?

10) Does everyone in the organization know to which business process they actively contribute?

11) Have performance measures for each process been established?

12) Have targets been set for each performance indicator?

13) Is performance being measured against the defined targets?

14) Are the changes to existing practices consistent with the governing requirements and the long term aims?

15) Have the characteristics for each process been identified?

Results

If satisfactory answers are obtained for all of the above questions, the conversion process is complete. Should any question receive a negative response, further design work is necessary but it may not be a barrier to proceeding with system construction in those areas that are ready. The final arbiter of success is whether performance metrics are showing improvement. The simplest test is to review the trend and be able to explain the change using information generated by the process based QMS.

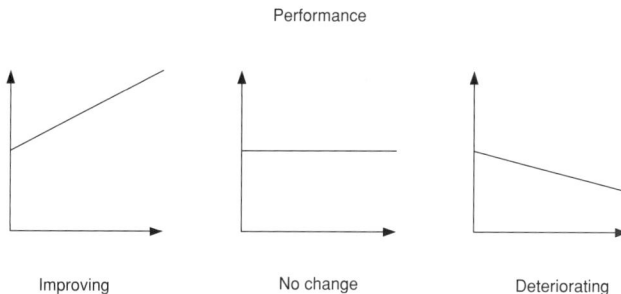

Performance

Improving | No change | Deteriorating

The past has only got us to where we are today
....it may not necessarily get us to where we want to be!

Appendix A

Sample flow charts for business processes

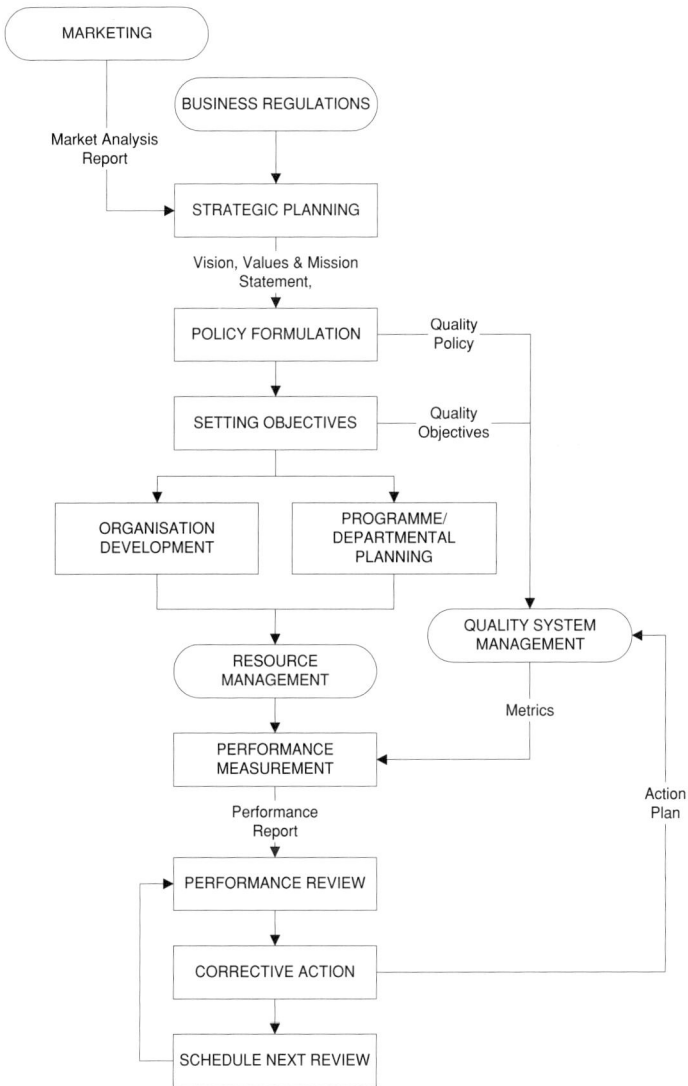

Figure A.1 Business management process

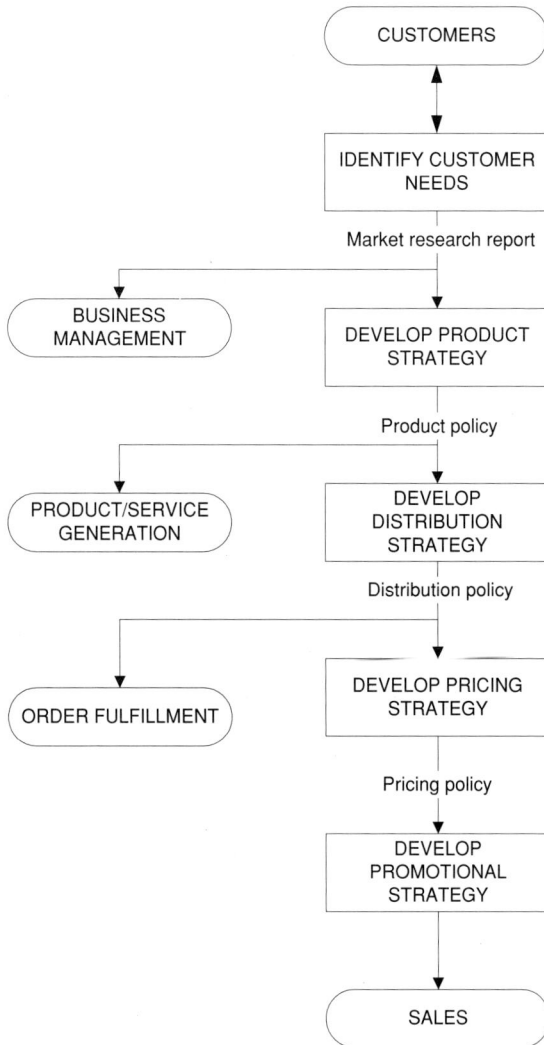

Figure A2 Marketing process

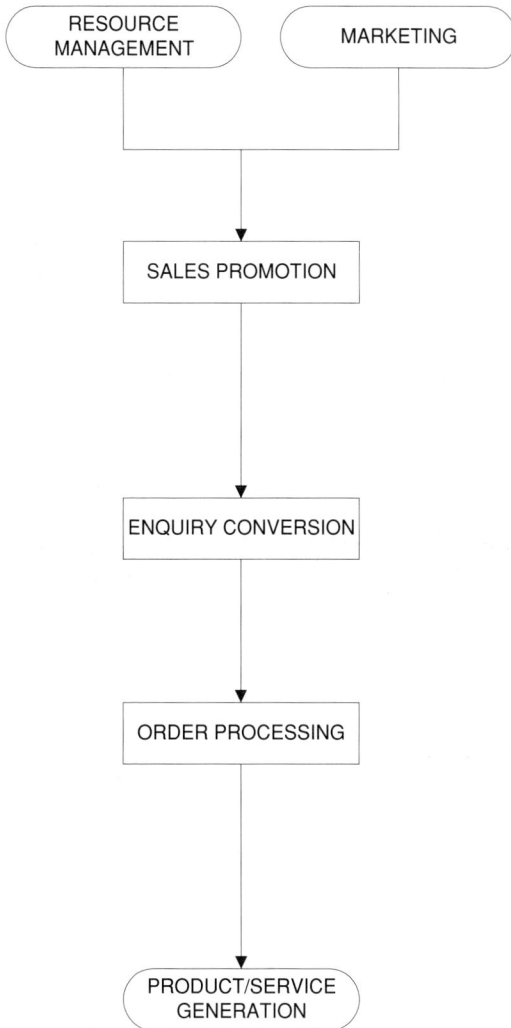

Figure A.3 Sales process

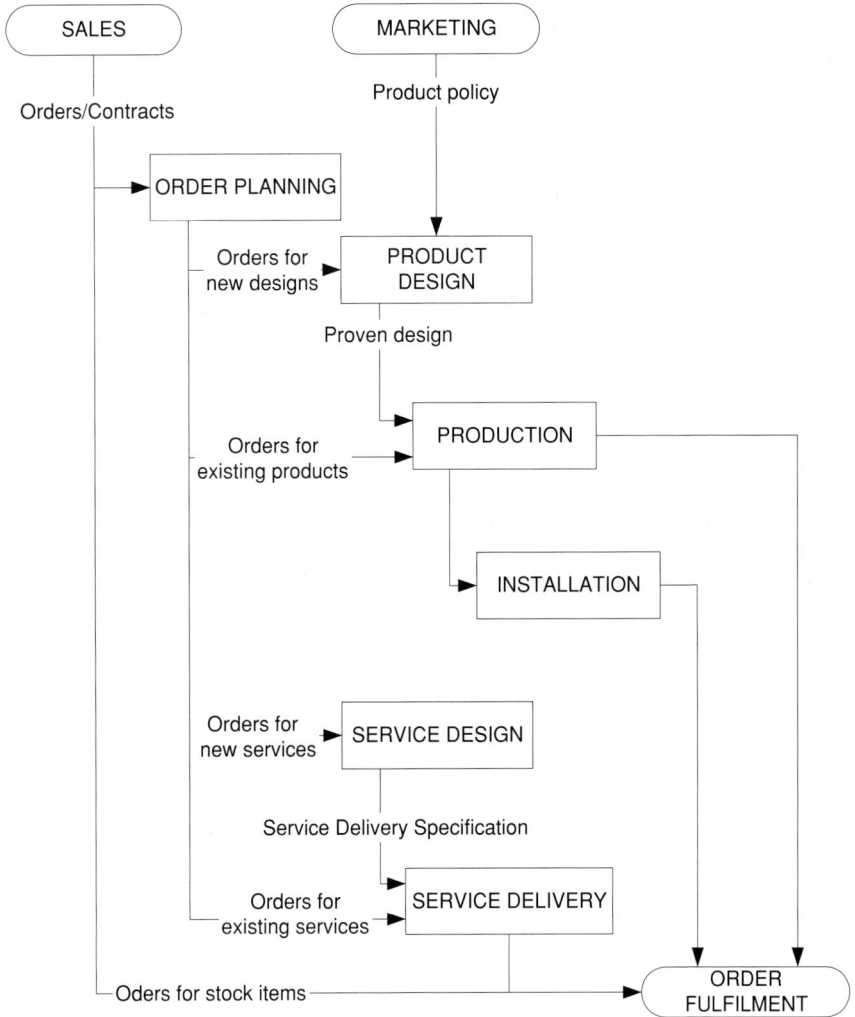

Figure A.4 Product/service generation process

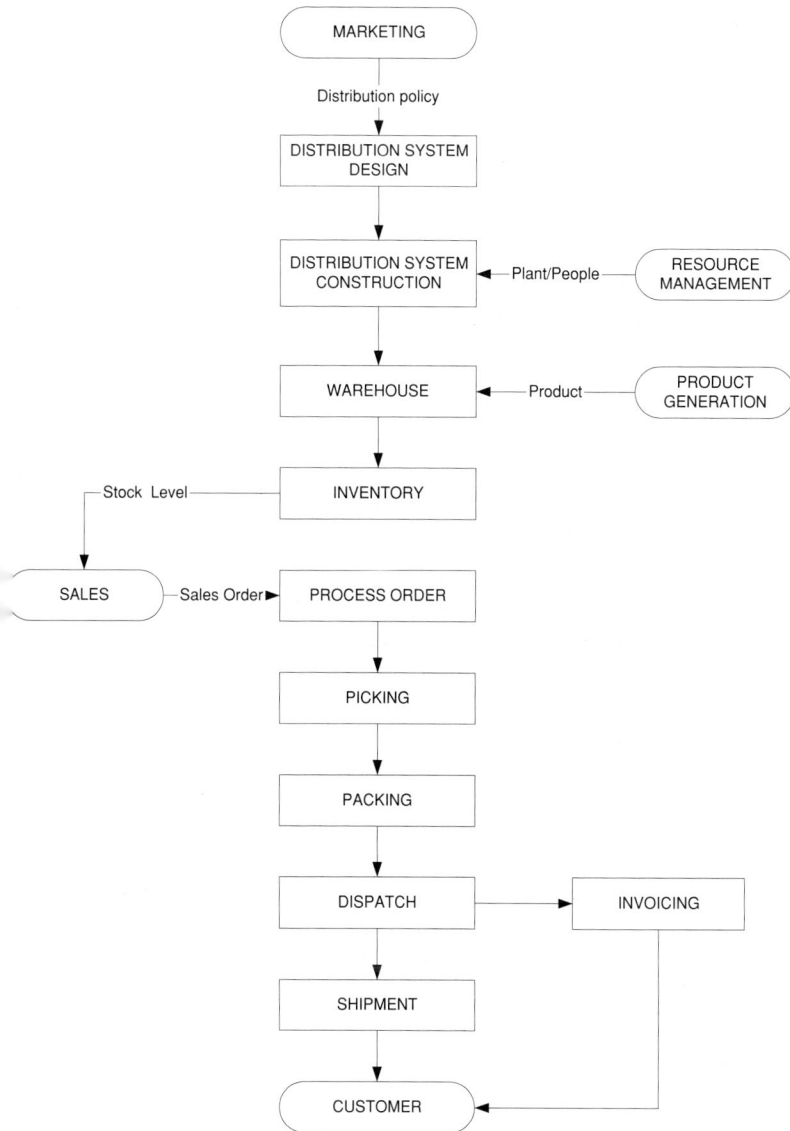

Figure A.5 Order fulfilment process

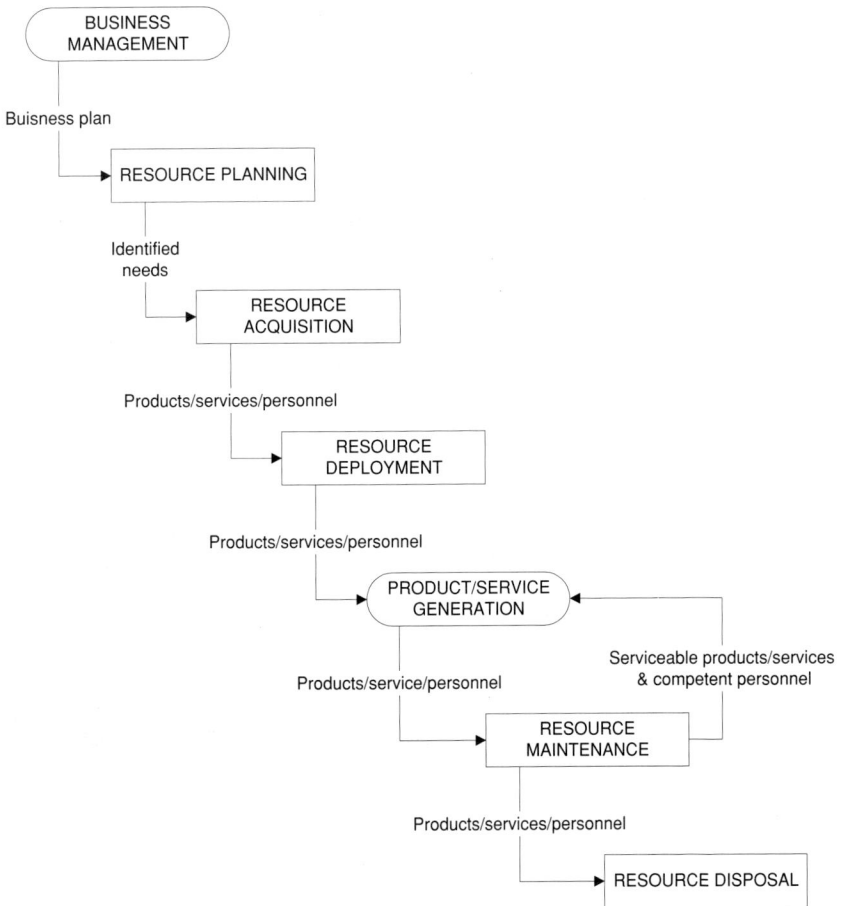

Figure A.6 Resource management process

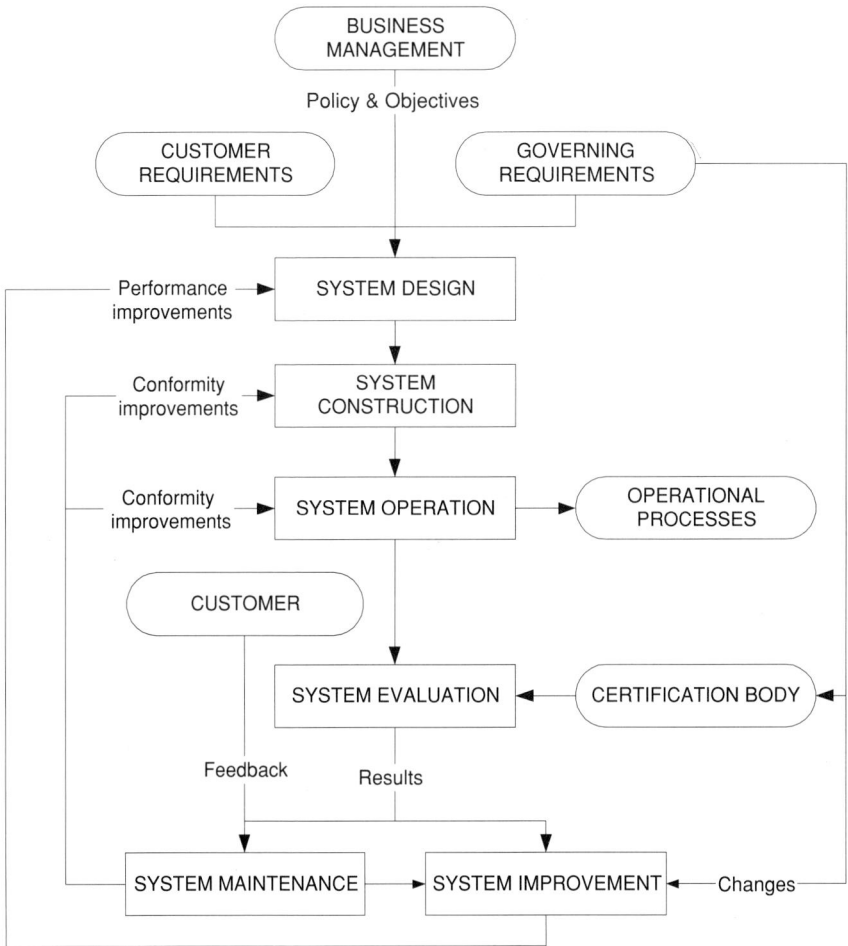

Figure A.7 QMS Management process

Appendix B

Sample flow charts for work processes

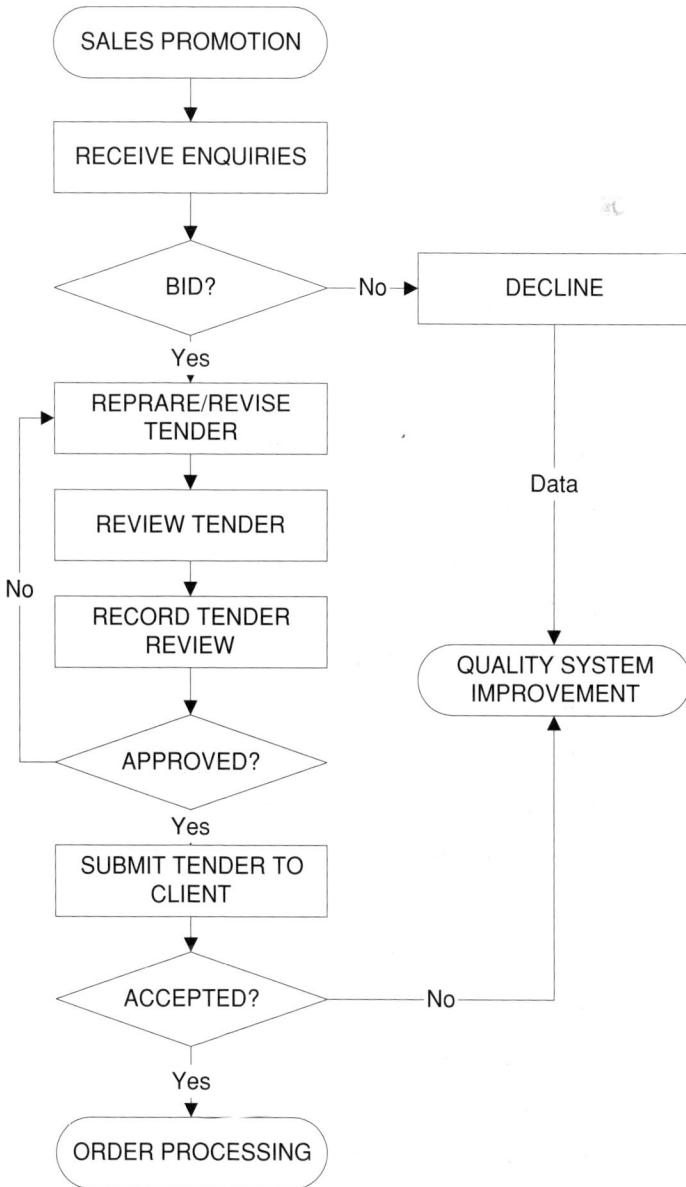

Figure B.1 Enquiry conversion process

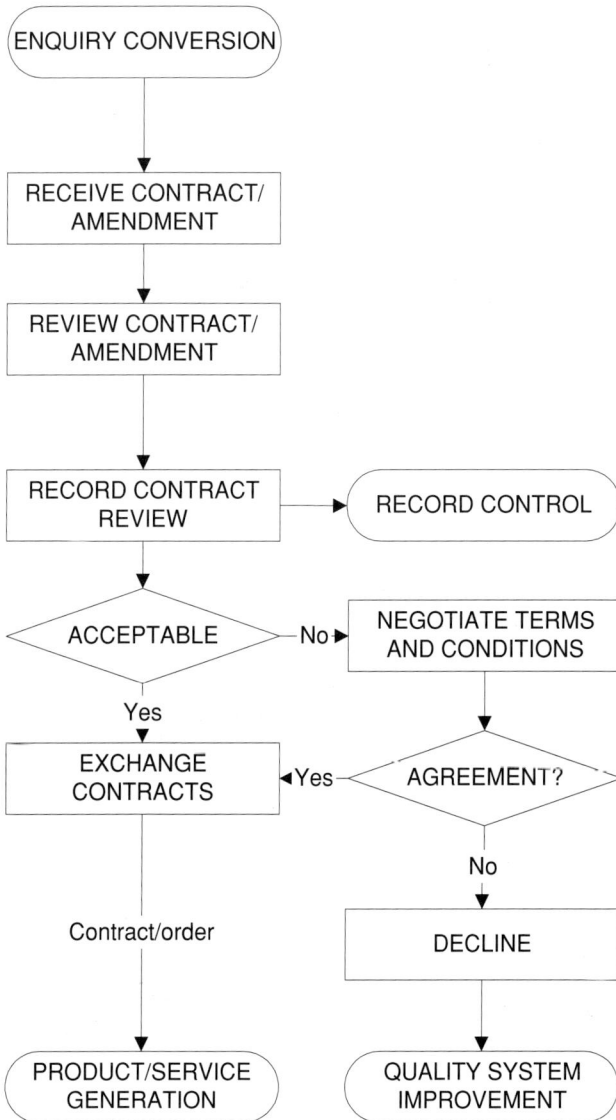

Figure B.2 Order processing process

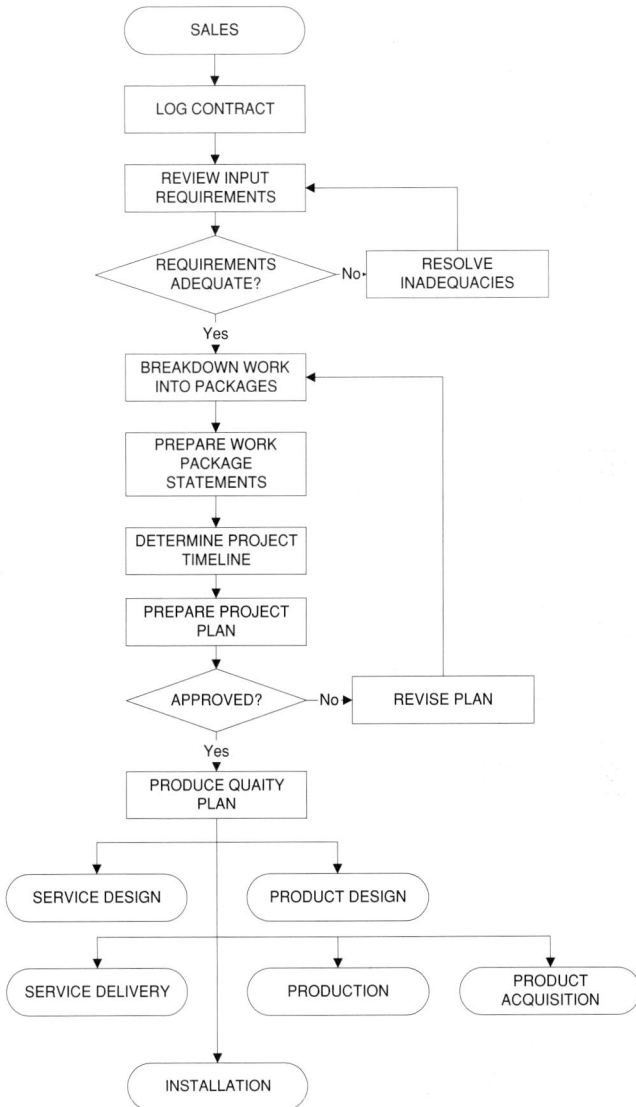

Figure B.3 Order planning process

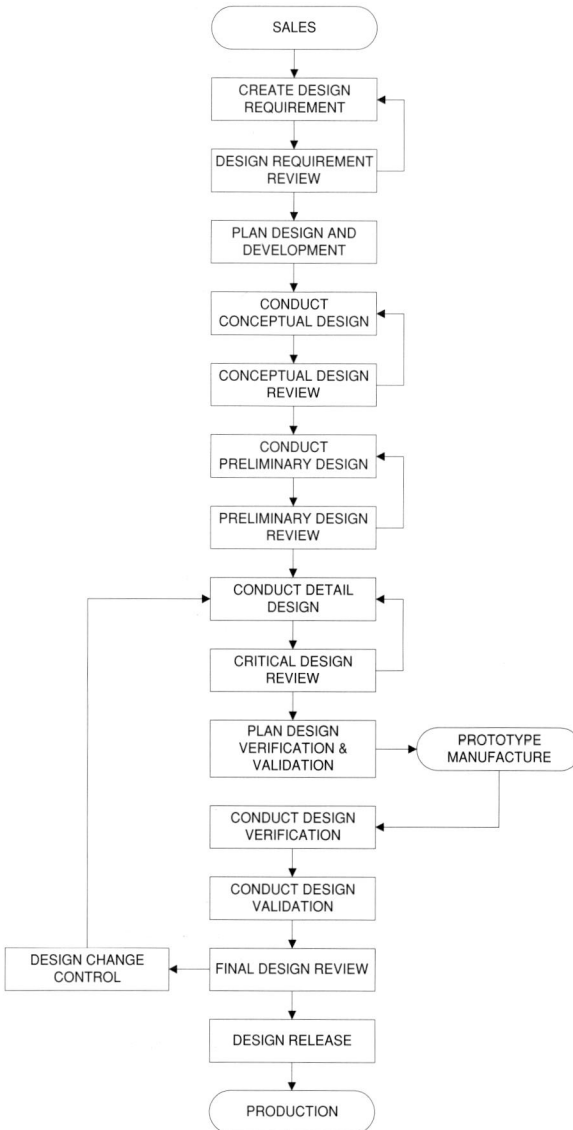

Figure B.4 Product design process

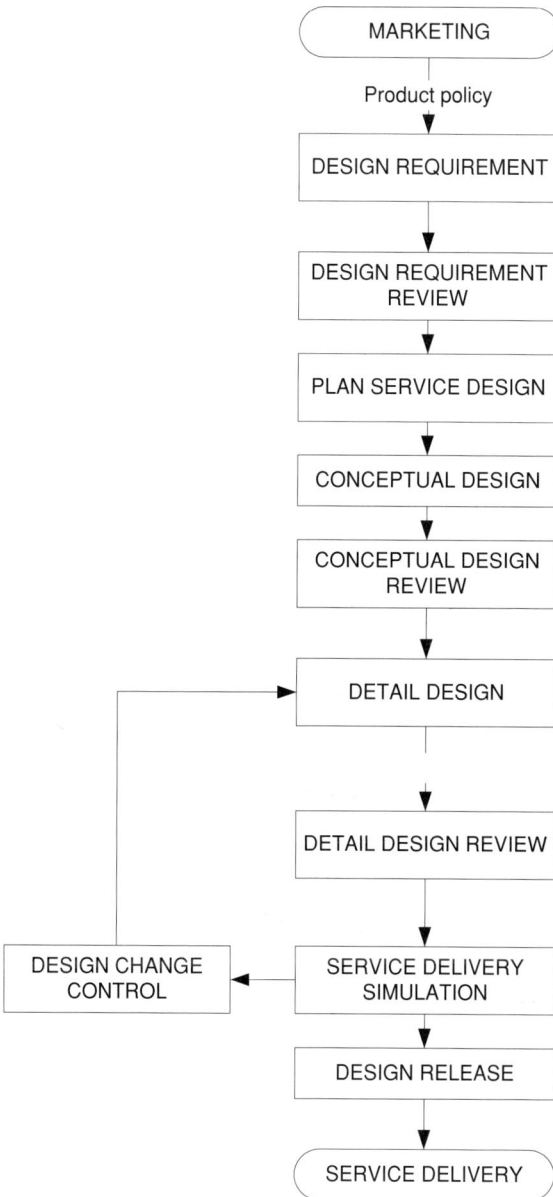

Figure B.5 Service design process

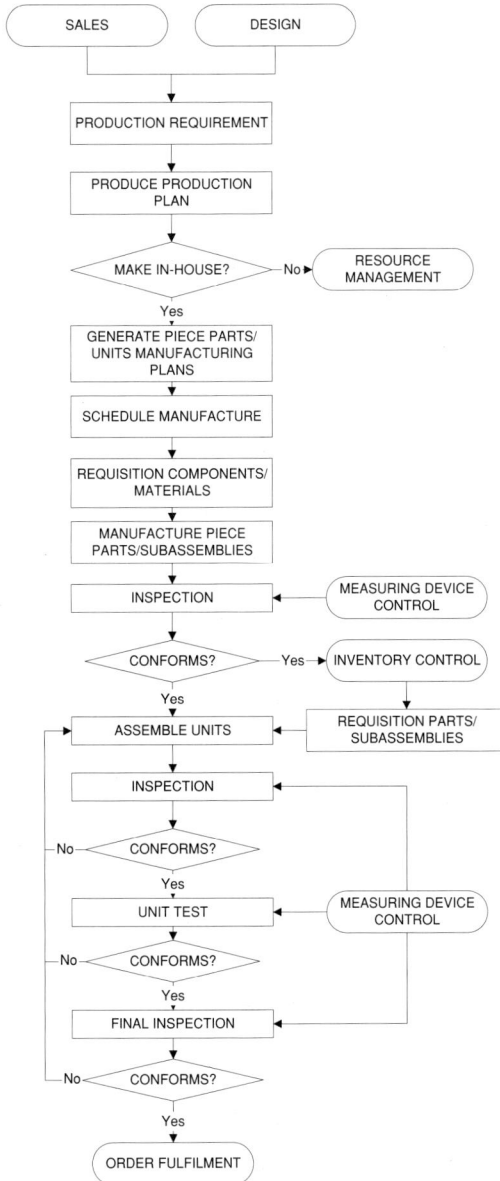

Figure B.6 Product manufacturing process

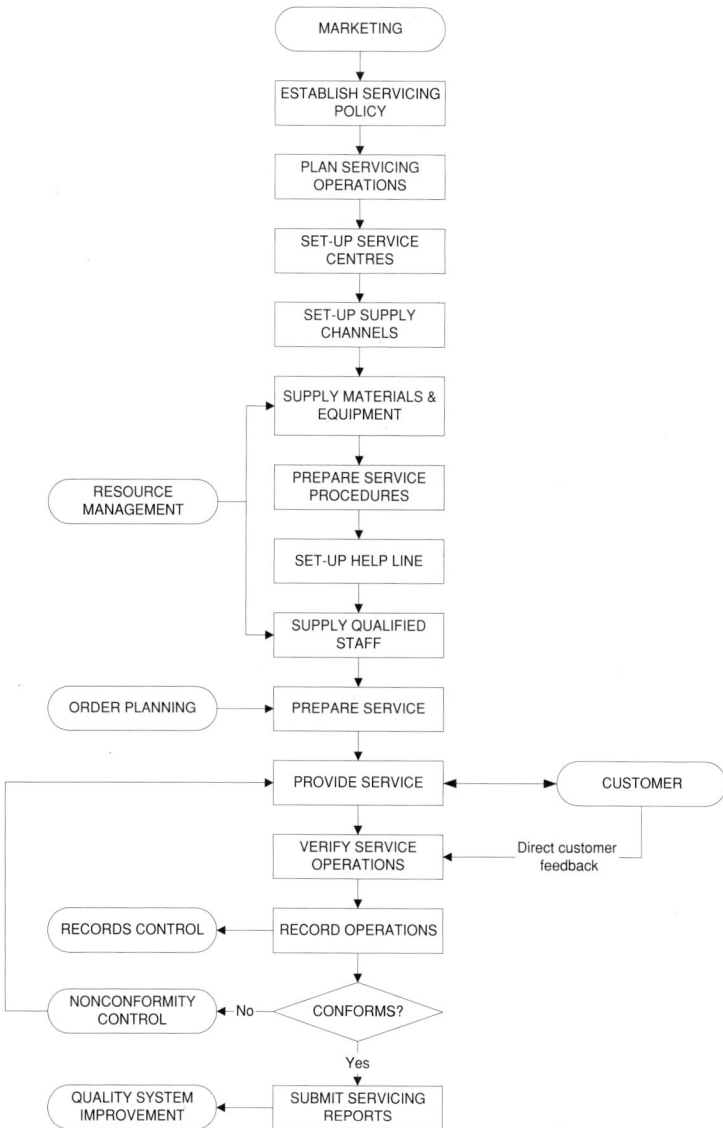

Figure B.7 Service delivery process

```
        ┌─────────────────────┐
        │   ORDER PLANNING    │
        └─────────────────────┘
                   │
                   ▼
        ┌─────────────────────┐
        │    SURVEY SITE      │
        └─────────────────────┘
                   │
                   ▼
        ┌─────────────────────┐
        │ DESIGN INSTALLATION │
        └─────────────────────┘
                   │
                   ▼
        ┌─────────────────────┐
        │  PLAN INSTALLATION  │
        └─────────────────────┘
                   │
                   ▼
        ┌─────────────────────┐
        │    PREPARE SITE     │
        └─────────────────────┘
                   │
                   ▼
        ┌─────────────────────┐        ┌──────────────────────┐
        │  DELIVER MATERIALS  │◄───────│  INVENTORY CONTROL   │
        └─────────────────────┘        └──────────────────────┘
                   │                              ▲
                   ▼                              │
        ┌─────────────────────┐                  │
        │  ENTRY INSPECTION   │                  │
        └─────────────────────┘                  │
                   │                              │
                   ▼                              │
             ◇ CONFORMS? ◇────────►┌──────────────────────┐
                   │          No   │   RETURN TO SOURCE   │
                  Yes             └──────────────────────┘
                   ▼
        ┌─────────────────────┐
        │   STORE MATERIALS   │
        └─────────────────────┘
                   │
                   ▼
        ┌─────────────────────┐
        │    INSTALLATION     │
        └─────────────────────┘
                   │
                   ▼
        ┌─────────────────────┐
        │    COMMISSIOING     │
        └─────────────────────┘
                   │
                   ▼
        ┌─────────────────────┐
        │     ACCEPTANCE      │
        └─────────────────────┘
                   │
                   ▼
             ◇ CONFORMS? ◇── No ►┌──────────────────────┐
                   │             │   NONCOMFORMITY      │
                  Yes            │     CONTROL          │
                   ▼             └──────────────────────┘
        ┌─────────────────────┐
        │   REMOVE SURPLUS    │
        └─────────────────────┘
                   │
                   ▼
        ┌─────────────────────┐
        │    HANDOVER TO      │
        │     CUSTOMER        │
        └─────────────────────┘
```

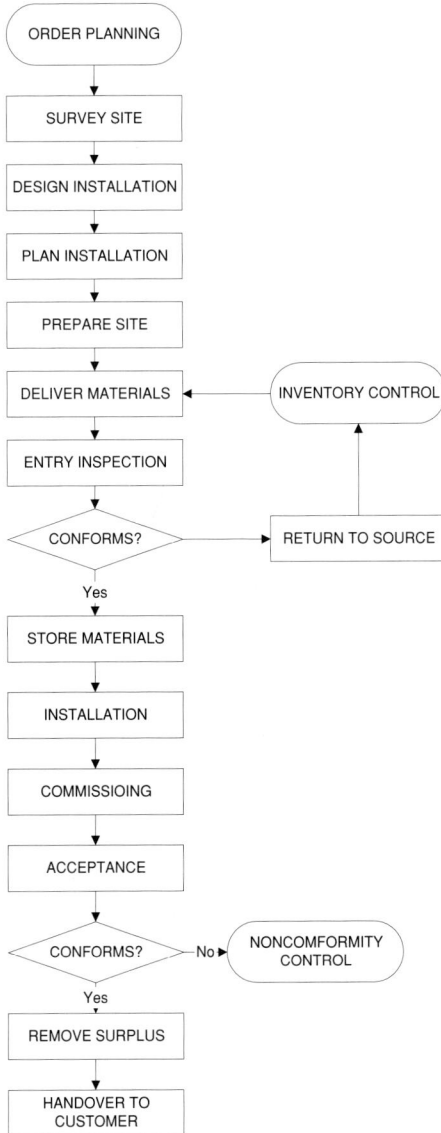

Figure B.8 Installation process

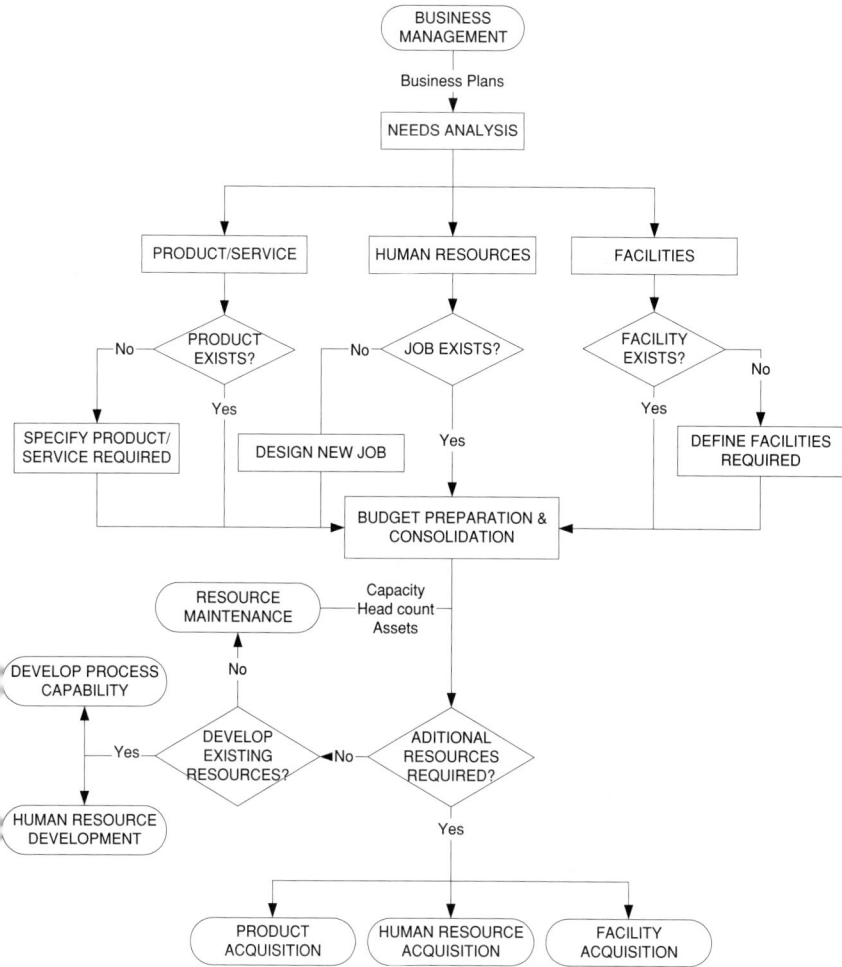

Figure B.9 Resource planning process

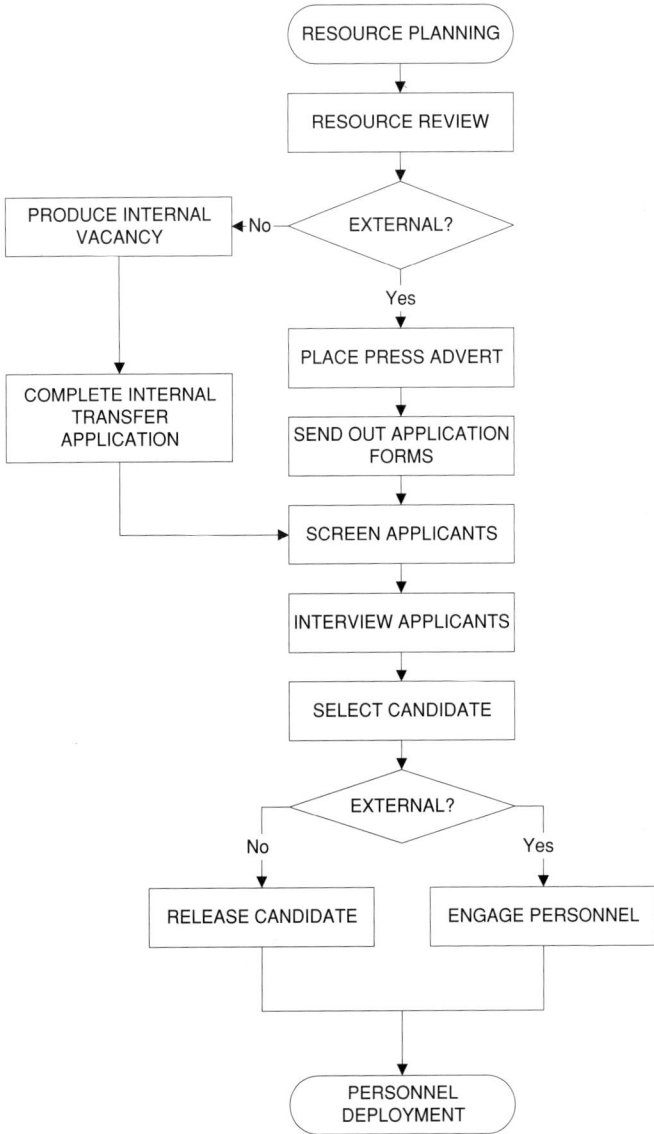

Figure B.10 Human resource acquisition process

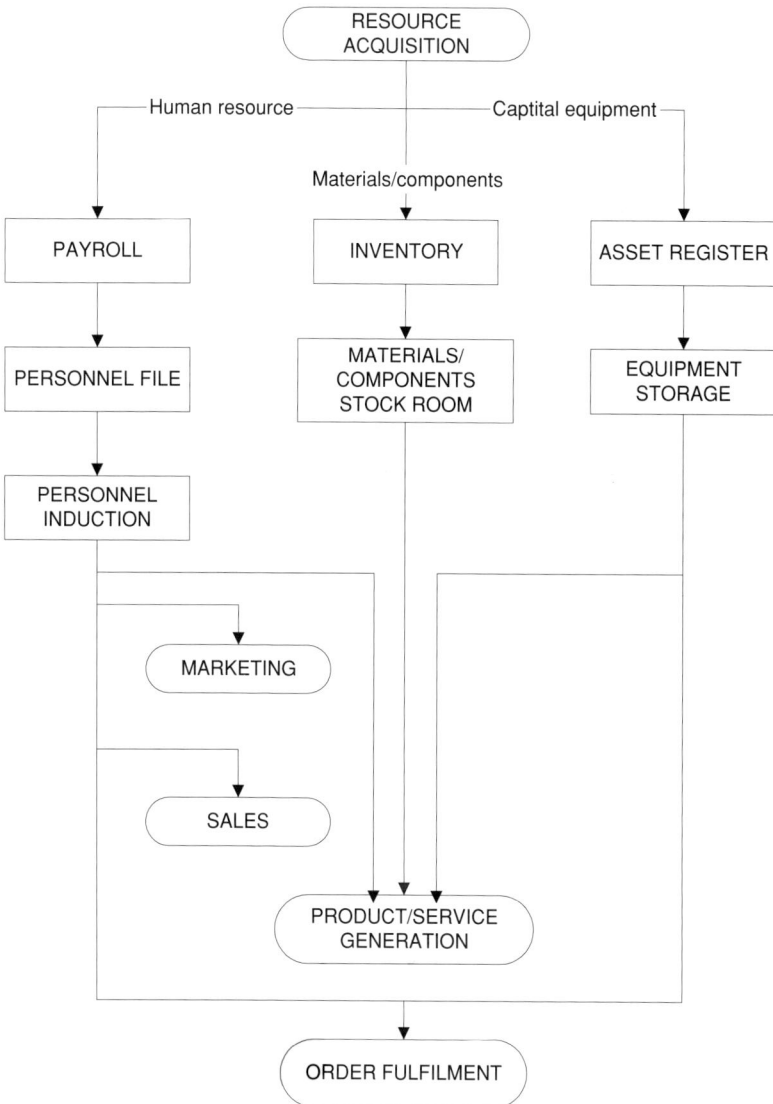

Figure B.11   *Resource deployment process*

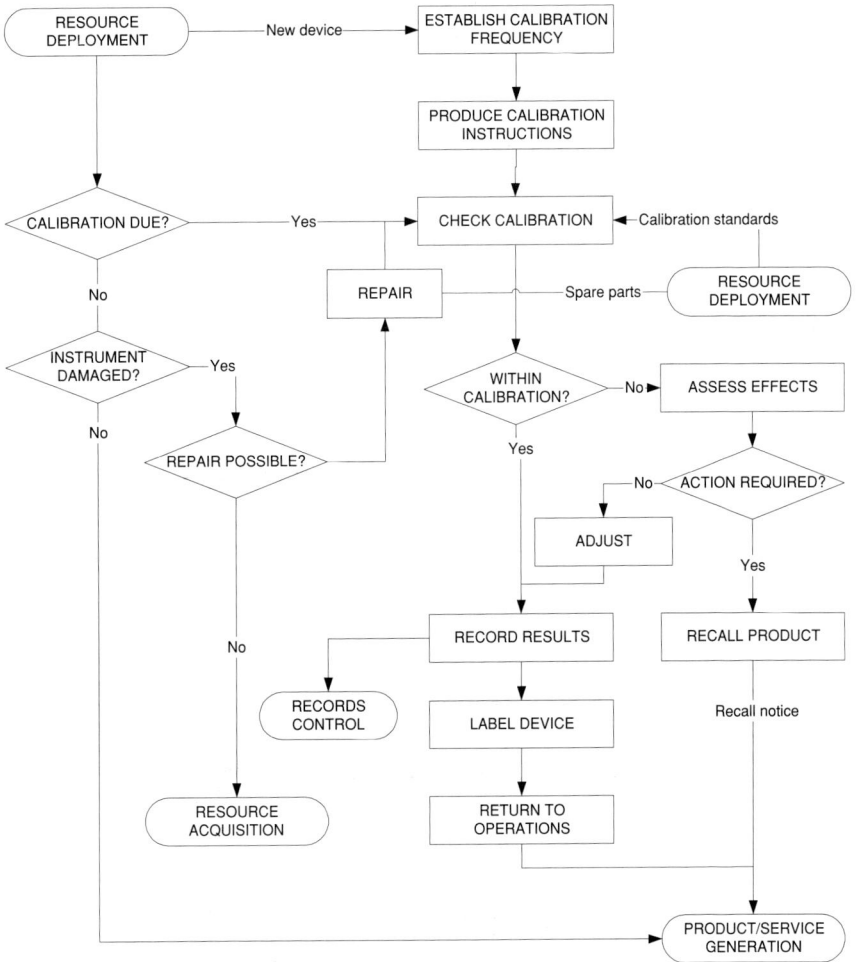

Figure B.12 Measuring device maintenance process

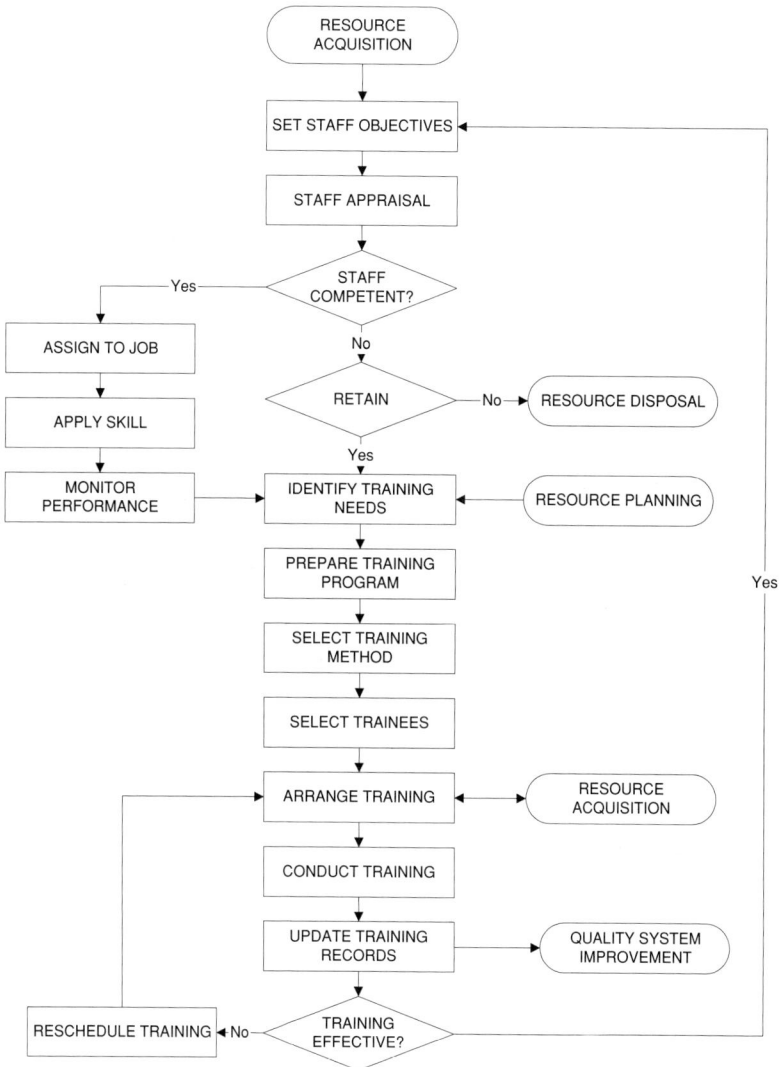

Figure B.13 Human resource development process

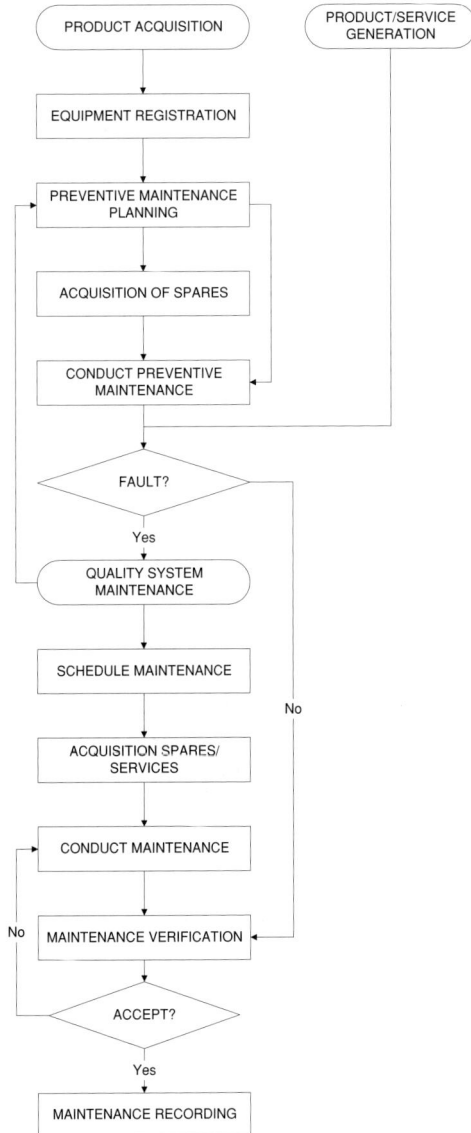

Figure B.14 Facility maintenance process

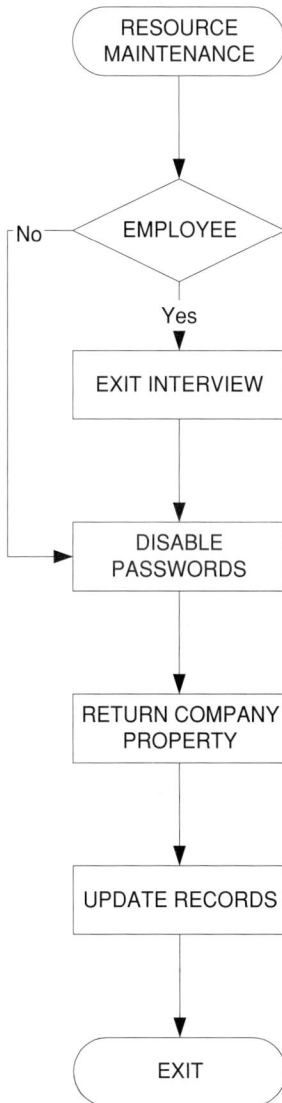

Figure B.15 Human resource termination process

```
        ╭─────────────────────╮
        │  RESOURCE           │
        │  MAINTENANCE        │
        ╰─────────────────────╯
                  │
                  ▼
        ┌─────────────────────┐
        │   DISPOSITION       │
        └─────────────────────┘
                  │
                  ▼
        ┌─────────────────────┐
        │   DISPOSAL          │
        │   REQUISITION       │
        └─────────────────────┘
                  │
                  ▼
        ┌─────────────────────┐
        │   DISPOSAL          │
        │   INSTRUCTIONS      │
        └─────────────────────┘
                  │
                  ▼
        ┌─────────────────────┐
        │ PREPARE EQUIPMENT   │
        │ FOR DISPOSAL        │
        └─────────────────────┘
                  │
                  ▼
        ┌─────────────────────┐
        │ TERMINATE SUPPORT   │
        │ CONTRACTS           │
        └─────────────────────┘
                  │
                  ▼
        ┌─────────────────────┐
        │  UPDATE RECORDS     │
        └─────────────────────┘
                  │
                  ▼
        ┌─────────────────────┐
        │   PACKING           │
        └─────────────────────┘
                  │
                  ▼
        ┌─────────────────────┐
        │   SHIPMENT          │
        └─────────────────────┘
                  │
                  ▼
        ╭─────────────────────╮
        │      EXIT           │
        ╰─────────────────────╯
```

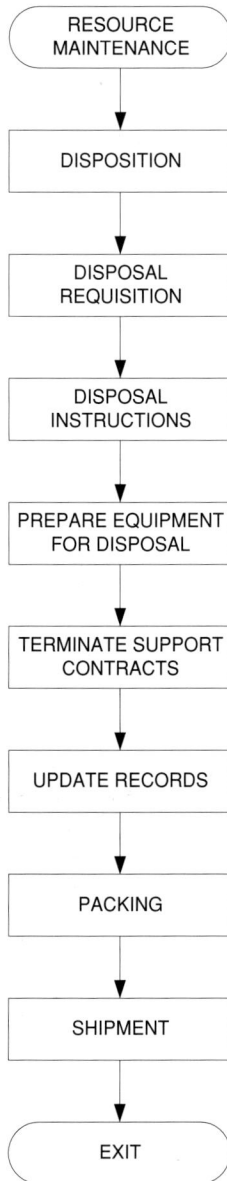

Figure B.16 Equipment disposal process

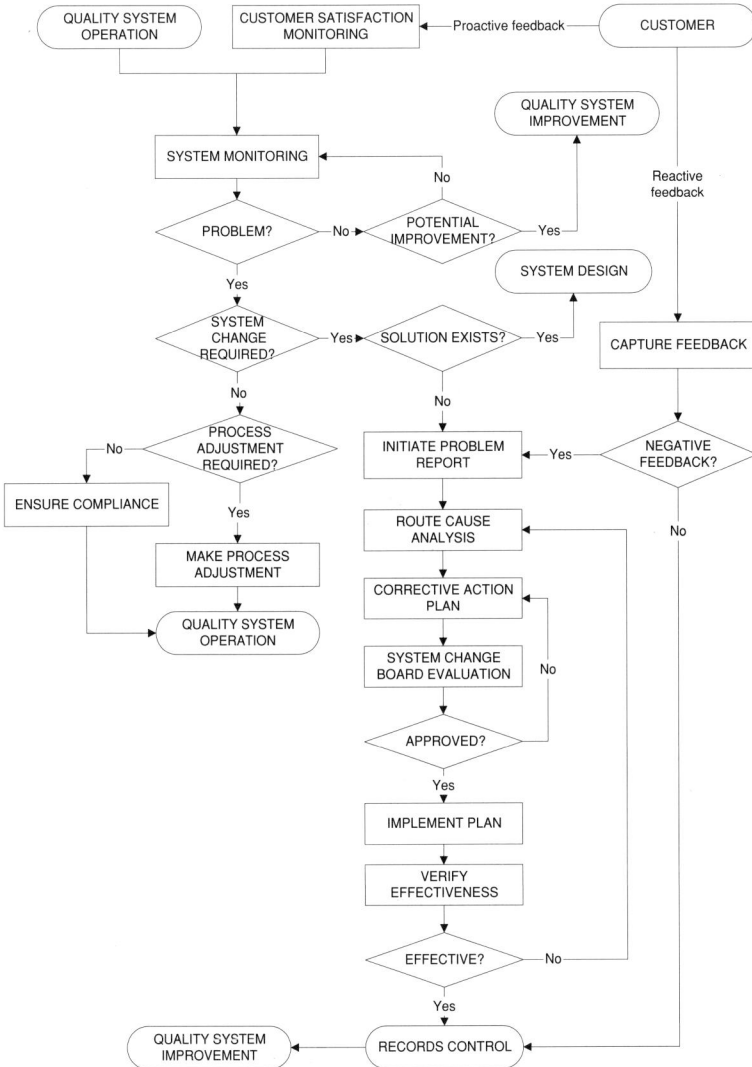

Figure B.17 QMS maintenance process

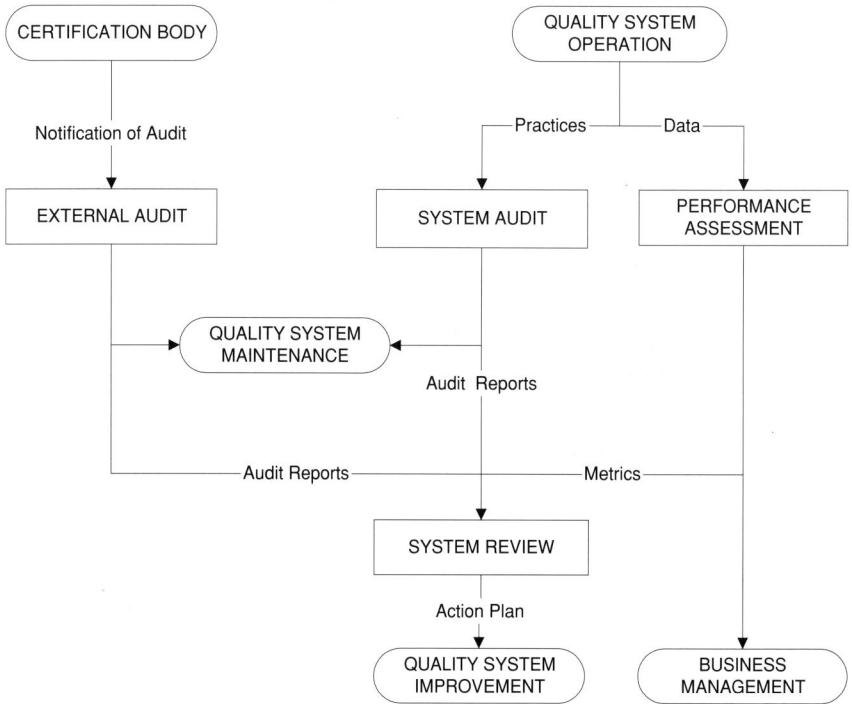

Figure B.18 QMS evaluation process

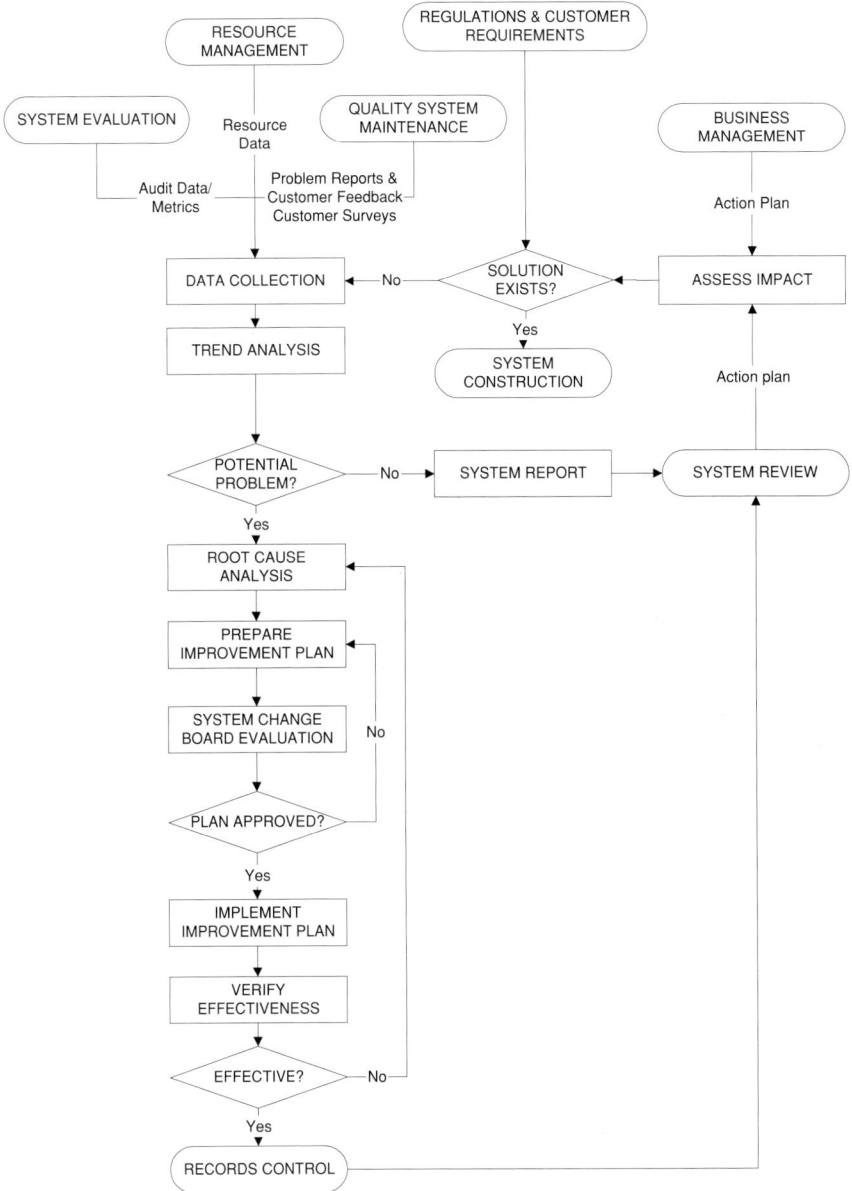

Figure B.19 QMS improvement process

About Transition Support

You can find out more from our web site http://www.transition.support.com

About the authors

The guide has been prepared by David Hoyle and John Thompson of Transition Support Ltd. David Hoyle has published several books on ISO 9000 and assisted many organizations achieve ISO 9000 registration using the process approach. John Thompson is a trained EFQM Assessor and has also assisted many organizations achieve ISO 9000 registration using the process approach.

Other publications from Transition Support

❑ Quality management principles ~ Self assessment

❑ ISO 9001:1994 to ISO 9001:2000 Analysis

❑ ISO/TS 16949 Gap Analysis

❑ ISO/TS 16949 Compliance Table ~Basic version

❑ ISO/TS 16949 Compliance Table ~Full version

❑ ISO 9001:1994 Auditor Questions

❑ ISO/TS 16949 to ISO 9001:2000 Analysis

❑ ISO 9001:2000 Auditor Questions

Other services from Transition Support

❑ ISO 9000:2000 Workshops

❑ Technical publishing

❑ Management consultancy

Feedback

We would welcome feedback from readers about this book and suggestions for improvement. You can contact us in the following ways:-

Tel/Fax: 00 44 (0)1600 716509 or 00 44 (0)1242 525859

E-mail: mail@transition-support.com

S-mail: Our mailing address is on page ii.